How To Make Money Buying Pre-Foreclosure Properties Before They Hit The County Courthouse Steps

The Complete Guide To Finding And Buying Pre-Foreclosure Properties

By Thomas J. Lucier

Fourth Edition
Second Printing

Published By Special Report Publications, LLC

Tampa, Florida
2003

How To Make Money Buying Pre-Foreclosure Properties Before They Hit The County Courthouse Steps

The Complete Guide To Finding And Buying Pre-Foreclosure Properties

By Thomas J. Lucier

Published by Special Report Publications, LLC
E-Mail: tomlucier@specialreportpubs.com
Telephone: (813) 237-6267
322 Rio Vista Court
Tampa, FL 33604-6941

Copyright © 1989, 1991, 2002, 2003 Thomas J. Lucier
ISBN 0-945343-06-X
Library of Congress Catalog Card Number 86-091868
Fourth Edition.
Second Printing.
All Rights Reserved.

No part of this publication may be reproduced or transmitted in any form or by any means, electronic or mechanical, including photocopying, recording or by any information storage and retrieval system, without written permission from the author, except for the inclusion of brief quotations in a review.

Table Of Contents

Dedication---To Dr. Jeffrey Lant……………………………………………………...1

About The Author---Thomas J. Lucier……………………………………………2

Preface………………………………………………………………………………..3

Publisher's Disclaimer Statement………………………………………………4

Introduction---Why I Wrote This Book, What's In And How To Use It………5

Chapter One---What You Need To Know About Buying Pre-Foreclosure Properties…………………………………………………………………………..9

Chapter Two---How To Properly Prepare Your Purchase Agreements And Protect Your Interests When Buying Pre-Foreclosure Properties……………..15

Chapter Three---How To Use Foreclosure Notices To Find Property Owners Whose Loans Are In Default And Facing Foreclosure…………………………23

Chapter Four---How To Contact Property Owners Whose Loans Are In Default And Facing Foreclosure………………………………………………….31

Chapter Five---How To Perform Due Diligence On Pre-Foreclosure Properties…………………………………………………………………………..43

Chapter Six---What You Need To Know About Real Estate Loans, Loan Covenants, Assumption Rules And Taking Title "Subject To" When Buying Pre-Foreclosure Properties………………………………………………………..55

Chapter Seven---How To Quickly Verify Loan Information With Foreclosing Lenders……………………………………………………………………………..63

Chapter Eight---How To Conduct A Thorough Property Inspection………..67

Chapter Nine---How To Accurately Estimate The Current Market Value Of A Pre-Foreclosure Property…………………………………………………………83

Chapter Ten---How To Negotiate With Property Owners Whose Loans Are In Default And Facing Foreclosure………...………………………………….……89

Chapter Eleven---How To Get Subordinate Lienholders To Discount Their Liens By Fifty Percent Or More………...……………………………………......95

Chapter Twelve---Everything You Need To Know About Short Payoff Sales: What They Are, How They Work And When To Use Them……...…………….101

Chapter Thirteen---How To Fix-Up Pre-Foreclosure Properties For Maximum Curb Appeal And Resale Value…………...….………………….115

Chapter Fourteen---How To Package, Market And Resell Pre-Foreclosure Properties For Maximum Profit…….....…………………………………….121

Resources……………………………………………………………………...131

Reader Review Form…....………………………………………………...137

Order Form……………………………………………………………...139

Dedication

How To Make Money Buying Pre-Foreclosure Properties Before They Hit The County Courthouse Steps is dedicated to Dr. Jeffrey Lant. I want to take this opportunity to give a very special heart felt thanks to Dr. Jeffrey Lant. Jeffrey's the copywriting genius who helped me develop my very successful method of using direct mail to contact property owners, whose loans are in default and facing foreclosure.

About The Author

Thomas J. Lucier is the President and CEO of Home Equities Corp, a privately held Florida Corporation established in 1995, that specializes in the purchase, fast-turnaround and resale of small residential rental properties in the Tampa Bay Area.

Mr. Lucier has owned residential and commercial rental property in the Tampa Bay Area since 1980, when he bought his first two rental houses while stationed in the Federal Republic of Germany with the United States Army.

Tom holds an active Florida Mortgage Broker License.

The award-winning Web site, www.floridalandlord.com, The One-Stop Cybersource For Florida's Do-It-Yourself Landlords And Property Management Professionals, is the "brainchild" of Thomas J. Lucier.

Mr. Lucier is also the managing member of Special Report Publications, LLC, the publisher of this book.

No "Johnny-come-lately" to the real estate investment information and advice business, Tom is the author of **The Florida Landlord's Manual, How To Use Real Estate Options To Control Undervalued Property, How To Buy Used And Bruised Houses For Fast Profits, How To Find, Buy And Turnaround Small, Mismanaged Rental Properties For Maximum Profit, How To Make Money Buying Pre-Foreclosure Properties Before They Hit The County Courthouse Steps** and **How To Quickly Evict A Residential Tenant In Florida**.

Mr. Lucier was the editor and publisher of **Distressed Property Investor's Monthly**, an eight-page newsletter that focused on the purchase, turnaround and resale of distressed property. **Distressed Property Investor's Monthly** later became a monthly feature in **Creative Real Estate Magazine**, where Tom was an associate editor.

In the early 1990s, Tom's weekly real estate investment advice column, **Tricks Of The Trade**, ran in newspapers in Philadelphia, Seattle, Charlotte, San Francisco, Cleveland, Oakland, Jacksonville, San Diego and Los Angeles.

Tom is an active member of the **National Association Of Real Estate Editors**.

Tom is also a member of the **Real Estate Educators Association**.

Mr. Lucier graduated *Cum Laude* from the University of South Florida in Tampa, Florida with a Bachelor of Arts Degree.

Tom Lucier's irreverent, no-nonsense, politically-incorrect writing style, and dry New England sense of humor provides a refreshing respite from the dry, dull, boring pap being peddled by most publishers.

For more information about Tom Lucier's background and to view his "paperwork" online, please log onto www.homeequitiescorp.com and click on Thomas J. Lucier.

Preface

Before I wrote the first edition of *How To Make Money Buying Pre-Foreclosure Properties Before They Hit The County Courthouse Steps* in 1989, I was making time-consuming and costly mistakes. The mistakes were inevitable; no one had written a book on how to buy pre-foreclosure properties, so I had to learn the hard way from my own mistakes and first hand experiences. All of the advice that I received said: "buy property on the county courthouse steps after it has been foreclosed on." But I eventually learned to avoid those costly courthouse-bidding wars by buying directly from property owners whose mortgage loans were in default and facing foreclosure. And the book that didn't exist back in 1985, when I bought my first pre-foreclosure property, is now in its fourth revised edition.

The First Pre-Foreclosure Book Ever Published

When the first edition of *How To Make Money Buying Pre-Foreclosure Properties Before They Hit The County Courthouse Steps* was published in 1989, it was the first book ever written exclusively on how to buy properties directly from owners in foreclosure. It was also the first "foreclosure book" ever published that advocated the use of direct mail to contact property owners whose mortgage or deed of trust loans were in default and facing foreclosure.

This Newly Revised Fourth Edition Has Been Expanded To Fourteen Chapters

This newly revised fourth edition of *How To Make Money Buying Pre-Foreclosure Properties Before They Hit The County Courthouse Steps*, has been expanded from twelve to fourteen chapters, and now includes chapters on the much-ballyhooed short payoff sale acquisition technique, and how to negotiate discounts with subordinate--junior--lienholders. This newly revised fourth edition also comes complete with step-by-step instructions, ready-to-use worksheets, checklists, sample agreements, Web site listings and a heavy dose of practical, no-nonsense advice on how to find and buy properties directly from owners whose mortgage or deed of trust loans are in default and facing foreclosure. Plus, you also get sample copies of six letters that you can use to contact property owners in foreclosure.

Knowledge And Persistence Are The Keys To Being A Profitable Investor

Contrary to popular belief, you don't need a degree from Harvard Law School in order to make money buying properties directly from owners whose mortgage or deed of trust loans are in default, and about to be sold at a public foreclosure auction or trustee's sale. Don't get me wrong, finding, researching, inspecting, negotiating, buying and reselling pre-foreclosure properties is a lot of hard work. But it can be a very lucrative line of work if you really know what you're doing, are well organized, and have the persistence that's necessary to be a profitable investor.

My Usual Warning

Lastly, unlike the roving real estate carnies, late-night, cable-television hucksters, Internet real estate whiz kids, and a certain Harvard Business School graduate posing as a "real estate savant," I don't claim to know-it-all, and you'll never hear me promise to make you a pre-foreclosure property millionaire within the next thirty days. I hate to be a spoilsport, but the simple fact remains that no real estate investment strategy will work unless you do!

Publisher's Disclaimer Statement

How To Make Money Buying Pre-Foreclosure Properties Before They Hit The County Courthouse Steps is written to provide accurate, authoritative information in regard to the subject matter covered. This information is made available with the understanding that the author, Thomas J. Lucier, and the publisher, Special Report Publications, LLC, are not engaged in the practice of rendering legal, accounting and financial advice. If legal, accounting and financial assistance are required, the services of properly licensed professionals should be sought.

Introduction

Why I Wrote This Book, What's In It And How To Use It

First off, I want to thank the thousands of people who invested their hard-earned money in a copy of the third edition of *How To Make Money Buying Pre-Foreclosure Properties Before They Hit The County Courthouse Steps*! I also want to thank you for buying a copy of this newly revised fourth edition! And, I also want to congratulate you on making a very wise investment decision! As you'll soon find out, this book lives up to its title. It's packed chock-full with step-by-step instructions, ready-to-use worksheets, checklists, sample letters and agreements, and practical, no-nonsense advice on how to buy properties directly from owners whose mortgage or deed of trust loans are in default and facing foreclosure. *How To Make Money Buying Pre-Foreclosure Properties Before They Hit The County Courthouse Steps* tells you precisely what to do, and exactly how to do it.

Why I Wrote This Newly Revised Fourth Edition

I wrote this newly revised fourth edition of *How To Make Money Buying Pre-Foreclosure Properties Before They Hit The County Courthouse Steps* to:
Reason #1: Improve, expand and update the information that was in the third edition of this book to better help readers take advantage of the many moneymaking opportunities that pre-foreclosure properties offer.
Reason #2: Alert and inform the public that because current economic conditions are causing overextended homeowners to default on their mortgage or deed of trust loans in record numbers, the coming months and years could provide numerous opportunities to buy properties at discounted prices directly from owners whose loans are in default and facing foreclosure.
Reason #3: Try and counteract the misinformation about pre-foreclosure and short payoff sale transactions, that's currently being foisted upon an unsuspecting public through the sale of overpriced "foreclosure" courses and boot camp seminars.

What You'll Find In This Book

How To Make Money Buying Pre-Foreclosure Properties Before They Hit The County Courthouse Steps is comprised of fourteen meaty chapters that are packed chock-full of step-by-step instructions, ready-to-use information and practical, no-nonsense advice. There's also an extensive resources section. Here's a brief outline of what you'll find in each chapter.

In chapter one, you'll learn what you need to know about buying pre-foreclosure properties. You'll also get the lowdown on exactly what you need to know about your state's foreclosure statute when buying properties directly from owners whose mortgage or deed of trust loans are in default and facing foreclosure.

Protecting your position, as buyer, is the subject covered in chapter two. You'll get the nitty-gritty details on how to properly prepare your purchase agreement when buying pre-foreclosure properties. You'll also get the inside scoop on how to fully protect your interests during the transaction. Please pay close attention to what's in this chapter so that you don't end up being sued by a seller claiming that you took "unfair advantage of their financial situation" when they were in foreclosure.

Chapter three tells you where foreclosure notices are filed in your county, and how to use them to find property owners whose mortgage or deed of trust loans are in default and facing foreclosure. You'll also get the lowdown on exactly how you can access your county's public records online to obtain information on foreclosure actions on the same day they're recorded in the official public records.

After you've finished reading chapter four, you'll know the methods that professionals use to contact property owners whose mortgage or deed of trust loans are in default. You also get sample copies of six different letters that you can use to contact property owners whose loans are in default and facing foreclosure.

In chapter five, you'll get a mini-course on how to perform due diligence on pre-foreclosure properties. You'll also learn how to use the Internet to access the numerous public records that are available online to find current information on a pre-foreclosure property and its owner.

Once you've finished reading chapter six, you'll know exactly what you need to know about real estate loans, loan covenants, assumption rules, taking title "subject to" and equity skimming when buying pre-foreclosure properties. This is extremely important stuff so make sure that you fully understand it.

Chapter seven provides you with complete details on how to work with foreclosing lenders to quickly verify loan information. You'll find out exactly who to ask for when contacting lenders about loans in default, so that you don't wind up dealing with some snotty loan clerk who doesn't know which way is up.

In chapter eight, you'll learn how to conduct a thorough pre-buy property inspection in order to avoid being bamboozled by an unscrupulous owner surreptitiously masking a property's major defects. This chapter also comes complete with ready-to-use checklists that you can use to conduct your own pre-buy property inspections.

By the time you've finished reading chapter nine, you'll know how to accurately estimate the current "as is" market value of a pre-foreclosure property. This is the single most important aspect of the entire buying process, so please make certain that you understand it before you go out on a buying binge!

Chapter ten gives you the step-by-step guidelines on how to negotiate with property owners whose mortgage or deed of trust loans are in default and facing foreclosure. You'll learn all of the little nuances about dealing with people who are usually in a constant state of denial about the imminent foreclosure on their property's loan.

In chapter eleven, you'll learn how to get subordinate or junior lienholders to discount their liens by fifty percent or more.

The much-ballyhooed short payoff sale acquisition technique is the subject matter of chapter twelve! You'll get step-by-step instructions and realistic advice on how to get lenders to agree to the short payoff of a mortgage or deed of trust loan.

How to fix-up pre-foreclosure properties for maximum curb appeal and resale value, is the subject covered in chapter thirteen. In this chapter, you'll find out how to give a pre-foreclosure property an industrial strength cleaning and cosmetic facelift on schedule and within budget.

The detailed information that you'll find in chapter fourteen will show you how to package, market and quickly resell pre-foreclosure properties for maximum profit. You'll get the lowdown on how to use the Internet to market your pre-foreclosure properties to a global audience.

In the resources section, you'll find a virtual cornucopia of reliable information sources that are available online at numerous real estate related Web sites. This extensive listing includes Internet public records sources where you can quickly find and verify property ownership, sales, tax assessment, environmental hazard, neighborhood crime and comparable sales data that you need to know about in order to make informed decisions.

Some Sage Advice That All Pre-Foreclosure Property Investors Should Follow

Here's five pieces of sage advice that all pre-foreclosure property investors should follow:
1. Concentrate on doing what you do best.
2. Understand that agreements are only as good as the people who sign them.
3. Assume nothing, verify everything and be prepared for anything.
4. Do what you say you're going to do when you say you're going to do it.
5. Realize that no real estate investment strategy will work unless you do.

Eight Reasons Why Most People Fail As Pre-Foreclosure Property Investors

As an author, I strive to always tell it to my readers as it really is. And I don't believe in sugarcoating the truth. That's why I want you to know right from the get-go, that most people--more than fifty-one percent--fail miserably as "pre-foreclosure property investors." I'm telling you this not to discourage you, but to forewarn you that buying properties directly from owners in foreclosure isn't as easy as many self-appointed "foreclosure experts and short sale pros" would like you to believe! I attribute this high failure rate to all of the hype, fairytales, half-truths, distortions and downright lies that most real estate hucksters use to sell overpriced "foreclosure" courses, and boot camp seminars. This type of misinformation is very misleading and creates unrealistic expectations on the part of the public!

And from my observations, most people who have unrealistic expectations usually fail as pre-foreclosure property investors, for one or more of the following eight reasons:

Reason #1: Lack of knowledge.
Reason #2: Failure to perform thorough due diligence inspections.
Reason #3: Lack of persistence.
Reason #4: Lack of capital and credit.
Reason #5: Lack of self-discipline.
Reason #6: Lack of people skills.
Reason #7: Failure to act in a timely manner.
Reason #8: Lack of an exit strategy.

Use This Book To Become Your Own Pre-Foreclosure Property Expert

Lastly, use this newly revised fourth edition of *How To Make Money Buying Pre-Foreclosure Properties Before They Hit The County Courthouse Steps* to educate yourself to the point that you become your own pre-foreclosure property expert. That's because you can't afford to blindly rely on the advice of other people who may or may not know what they're doing when it comes to buying pre-foreclosure properties. Even if they have experience with conventional real estate transactions, they may be totally clueless about how to solve the potential problems associated with buying pre-foreclosure properties. Let's face it, if you don't understand how the foreclosure process works in your state, how will you know if the person advising isn't full of what makes the grass grow greener? Quite simply, you won't. That's because if you can't confirm what you're being told to do, there's an excellent chance that you'll end up being what I call a "mushroom investor." That's an investor who's kept in the dark and fed a lot of bullspit by their "adviser, mentor or coach!"

Yours for profitable pre-foreclosure property investing,

Thomas J. Lucier

Tampa, Florida

Chapter One

What You Need To Know About Buying Pre-Foreclosure Properties

Typically, distressed property sales are forced sales conducted by foreclosing lenders, tax collectors, bankruptcy court trustees and government agencies in accordance with prescribed rules, regulations, statutes and procedures. However, when you buy properties directly from owners whose mortgage or deed of trust loans are in default and facing foreclosure, you become involved in a sort of "real estate free-for-all." A "free-for-all" in which, terms are negotiated one-on-one between sellers who usually begrudgingly sell as a last resort, and over-anxious buyers, who oftentimes don't really know what they're doing. One of the major problems in buying pre-foreclosure properties is that buyers lack the normal intermediaries they depend on in a conventional, easy-to-close real estate transaction. In a conventional real estate transaction between a willing seller and a willing buyer, real estate agents, title and escrow agents and attorneys, are readily available to hold hands and slowly walk both parties through the transaction. But this isn't the case when you buy a pre-foreclosure property that can have a myriad of unique problems that must be quickly solved before the property's loan is foreclosed on, and sold at a public foreclosure auction or trustee's sale. Plus, when you buy properties directly from owners in foreclosure, time is always of the essence. That's because when most owners in foreclosure finally decide to throw-in-the-towel, and sell their property, it's almost always at the eleventh hour in the foreclosure process, usually within a couple of days before the public foreclosure auction or trustee's sale is scheduled to take place.

Nothing Illegal Or Unethical About Buying Property From Owners In Foreclosure

First things first: In spite of what certain uninformed members of the media would want the American public to believe, there's nothing inherently illegal or unethical about buying properties directly from owners whose mortgage or deed of trust loans are in default and facing foreclosure. Fact is, honest, ethical, pre-foreclosure property investors provide much needed debt-relief to ten of thousands of financially distressed property owners annually.

The Definition Of Foreclosure

Foreclosure is generally defined as: *"A legal process through which property, pledged as security for a debt, a mortgage or deed of trust loan, is foreclosed on by the lender, because the borrower defaulted by failing to meet the repayment terms contained in the loan agreement and promissory note."*

What The Term "Pre-Foreclosure" Means

The term "pre-foreclosure" refers to the period of time between when a foreclosure lawsuit and notice of lis pendens, or a notice of default has been filed and recorded in the official public records, and the date of the scheduled public foreclosure auction or trustee's sale.

Why It's Best To Buy Properties Directly From Owners In Foreclosure

As far as I'm concerned, it's best to avoid public foreclosure auction and trustee's sales, and instead, buy properties directly from owners in foreclosure. This way you:
1. Have an opportunity to buy a property owner's equity at a discount of fifty percent or more.
2. Can inspect the property and estimate the repair costs.
3. Avoid the competitive bidding process that's a part of public foreclosure auction and trustee sales.
4. Eliminate the owners right to redeem the property after the sale.

Buying Properties from Owners In Foreclosure Requires Specialized Knowledge

The secret to being a profitable pre-foreclosure property investor is specialized knowledge. In no other type of distressed property investment is specialized knowledge so highly rewarded and ignorance so harshly punished. In this business, you can't afford to blindly rely on the "expertise and advice" of so-called "real estate professionals" such real estate agents, title and escrow agents and attorneys who may or may not know what they're doing when it comes to fully understanding the process of buying properties directly from owners in foreclosure. And if you don't know the mechanics of how the foreclosure process works in your state, how will you know if the person advising you knows it any better? Quite simply, you won't. That's why it's imperative that before you ever go out on a pre-foreclosure property-buying binge, you first know:
1. The type of foreclosure action that's used in your state to foreclose on residential loans.
2. How the judicial or nonjudicial foreclosure process works in your state.
3. The length of time that it takes to complete a foreclosure action in your state.
4. If your state's foreclosure statute gives homeowners the right to cancel a purchase agreement.

How To Find Your State's Foreclosure Statute Online

The quickest way to find your state's foreclosure statute online is to type the name of your state followed by the words "foreclosure statute" into a search engine like www.google.com. All state statutes are available online at the Web site listed below:
State Statutes
www.prairienet.org/~scruffy/f.htm

The Two Types Of Foreclosure Actions Used To Foreclose On Residential Loans

The two types of foreclosure actions used to foreclose on residential mortgage and deed of trust loans are:
1. Judicial foreclosure.
2. Nonjudicial foreclosure.

How The Judicial Foreclosure Process Works

In states where judicial foreclosure is used to foreclose on residential mortgage and deed of trust loans, the foreclosing lender files a lawsuit to foreclose, naming as defendant the defaulting borrower--mortgagor or trustor--and all lienholders of record having an interest in the property subsequent to the lender recording their mortgage or deed of trust. The defaulting borrower and other interested parties--defendants--are then summoned, that is, officially notified by the court of the lawsuit pending against the defaulting borrower. In addition, a notice of lis pendens--suit pending--is also filed with the county or public recorder's office to notify the general public that a lawsuit is pending against the property owner. Once notified, the borrower or any other defendant named in the lawsuit normally has twenty days to formally reply to the lawsuit and present their case. If no reply is made, or the judge rules against the defendant's reply, the judge then orders the mortgage or deed of trust loan to be foreclosed on, and the property sold at a public foreclosure auction sale to satisfy the foreclosing lender's claim. Here's a sequential outline of what happens under judicial foreclosure when a borrower defaults on a residential mortgage or deed of trust loan:

1. The lender files a lawsuit to foreclose the mortgage or deed of trust loan with a court of competent jurisdiction.
2. The borrower responds to the foreclosure lawsuit complaint and a court hearing date is set.
3. The Foreclosure lawsuit is heard in court and the judge either dismisses the case or orders the loan to be foreclosed on.
4. The judge rules against the defendant borrower and orders the loan to be foreclosed on, and that a public foreclosure auction sale date be scheduled for the property.
5. The public foreclosure auction sale is advertised.
6. The property is sold to highest bidder at a public foreclosure auction sale or taken back by the lender.
7. The judge may award the lender a deficiency judgment against the borrower, if the bid the lender accepted, was for less than the loan balance owed.
8. The borrower may exercise any statutory redemption rights after the sale.
9. A sheriff's deed or certificate of title is given to the highest bidder after any statutory redemption period expires.

How The Nonjudicial Foreclosure Process Works

In states where nonjudicial foreclosure is used to foreclose on residential mortgage and deed of trust loans, the foreclosing mortgage lender or deed of trust beneficiary invokes the power of sale covenant contained in the mortgage or deed of trust, which gives the lender, or the trustee holding the deed of trust, the right to foreclose the loan in default by filing a notice of default with the county or public recorder's office. Unlike the judicial foreclosure process, this is done without having to file a foreclosure lawsuit in court. Here's a sequential outline of what happens under nonjudicial foreclosure when a borrower defaults on a residential mortgage or deed of trust loan:

1. The trustee files a notice of default with the county or public recorder's office.
2. The public trustee's sale date is set.
3. The public trustee's sale is advertised.
4. The property is sold to highest bidder at a public trustee's auction sale, or taken back by the lender.
5. The borrower may exercise any statutory redemption rights after the sale.
6. A trustee's deed is given to the highest bidder after any statutory redemption rights have expired.

Know If Your State Has Any Type Of Home Equity Sales Contact Statute

Some states, most notably California, have home equity sales contract statutes which were enacted to prevent buyers from "taking unfair advantage" of homeowners in foreclosure by using high pressure sales tactics to get homeowners to sign a purchase agreement. Most home equity sales contract statutes specify that buyers making offers on owner-occupied one to four-unit residential properties, whose loans are in default, must include a right of rescission or notice of cancellation clause in their purchase agreements. This clause gives homeowners a period of time, usually five business days, excluding weekends and holidays, after the contract was signed, during which they can rescind or cancel the purchase agreement.

The Two Statutes That Regulate California Pre-Foreclosure Property Investors

The California State Legislature has enacted the following two statutes to try and protect homeowners in foreclosure from "fraud, deception and unfair dealing" by home equity purchaser's and foreclosure consultants:
1. California home equity sales contracts. California home equity sales contracts are covered under Sections 1695-1695.17 of the California Civil Code.
2. California mortgage foreclosure consultants. California mortgage foreclosure consultants are covered under Sections 2945-2945.11 of the California Civil Code.

The California Civil Code Is Available Online

The California Civil Code is available online at the following Web site:
California Civil Code
www.leginfo.ca.gov/calaw.html

Where To Find Reliable Information On The Foreclosure Process In Your State

The most reliable and up-to-date source of state-by-state foreclosure information that I've found is the ***Foreclosure Desk Guide***, that's published by the United States Foreclosure Network (USFN). The United States Foreclosure Network is a nonprofit association of law firms and trustee companies that provide loan loss mitigation and foreclosure services to the mortgage industry. The ***Foreclosure Desk Guide*** is what the members of the USFN use as their foreclosure reference guide. This cornucopia of foreclosure information covers everything from breach letters to foreclosure notices to subordinate liens, and is available at the United States Foreclosure Network Web site that's listed below:
United States Foreclosure Network
www.usfn.org

State-By-State Foreclosure Statutes

The following is a state-by-state listing of commonly used security instruments, foreclosure actions and the foreclosure statute number for each state:

State	Security Instrument	Foreclosure Action	Statute Number
Alabama	Mortgage	Nonjudicial	§35-10-1
Alaska	Deed of Trust	Nonjudicial	§34.20.090
Arizona	Deed of Trust	Nonjudicial	§33.807
Arkansas	Mortgage	Judicial	§51-1106
California	Deed of Trust	Nonjudicial	§2924
Colorado	Deed of Trust	Nonjudicial	§38-37-113
Connecticut	Mortgage	Strict Foreclosure	§49-24
Delaware	Mortgage	Judicial	§2101
District of Columbia	Deed of Trust	Nonjudicial	§45-701
Florida	Mortgage	Judicial	§702.01
Georgia	Security Deed	Nonjudicial	§44-14-162
Hawaii	Mortgage	Nonjudicial	§667-1
Idaho	Deed of Trust	Nonjudicial	§6-101
Illinois	Mortgage	Judicial	§15-101
Indiana	Mortgage	Judicial	§32-8-11-3
Iowa	Mortgage	Judicial	§654.1
Kansas	Mortgage	Judicial	§60-2410
Kentucky	Mortgage	Judicial	§381.190
Louisiana	Mortgage	Executive Process	§2631 - 2724
Maine	Mortgage	Judicial	§6321
Maryland	Deed of Trust	Nonjudicial	§7-101
Massachusetts	Mortgage	Judicial	§19.21
Michigan	Mortgage	Nonjudicial	§451.401
Minnesota	Mortgage	Nonjudicial	§500.01
Mississippi	Deed of Trust	Nonjudicial	§89-1-55
Missouri	Deed of Trust	Nonjudicial	§443.320
Montana	Deed of Trust	Nonjudicial	§71-1-228
Nebraska	Mortgage	Judicial	§25-2139
Nevada	Deed of Trust	Nonjudicial	§107.020
New Hampshire	Mortgage	Nonjudicial	§479.22
New Jersey	Mortgage	Judicial	§2A-50-2
New Mexico	Mortgage	Judicial	§48-7-7
New York	Mortgage	Judicial	§1301-91
North Carolina	Deed of Trust	Judicial	§45
North Dakota	Mortgage	Judicial	§32-19-01
Ohio	Mortgage	Judicial	§2323.07
Oklahoma	Mortgage	Judicial	§686
Oregon	Deed of Trust	Nonjudicial	§86.010
Pennsylvania	Mortgage	Judicial	§1141
Rhode Island	Mortgage	Nonjudicial	§34-11-22
South Carolina	Mortgage	Judicial	§15-7-10
South Dakota	Mortgage	Judicial	§21-47-1

Tennessee	Deed of Trust	Nonjudicial	§35-501
Texas	Deed of Trust	Nonjudicial	§51.002
Utah	Deed of Trust	Nonjudicial	§57-1-14
Vermont	Mortgage	Judicial	§4528
Virginia	Deed of Trust	Nonjudicial	§55-59.1
Washington	Deed of Trust	Nonjudicial	§61.12.010
West Virginia	Deed of Trust	Nonjudicial	§38-1-3
Wisconsin	Mortgage	Judicial	§846.01
Wyoming	Mortgage	Judicial	§1-18-101

State-By-State Foreclosure Timeline

The following is a state-by-state listing of the average length of time that it takes for a loan to be foreclosed on from the time a lender files a foreclosure lawsuit or records a notice of default, to the time a public foreclosure auction or trustee's sale takes place:

State	Number of Months	State	Number of Months
Alabama	Three	Montana	Six
Alaska	Four	Nebraska	Four
Arkansas	Three	Nevada	Four
Arizona	Three	New Hampshire	Three
California	Four	New Jersey	Ten
Colorado	Five	New Mexico	Five
Connecticut	Six	New York	Ten
Delaware	Seven	New Jersey	Ten
District of Columbia	Four	North Dakota	Four
Florida	Seven	Ohio	Eight
Georgia	Three	Oklahoma	Seven
Hawaii	Seven	Oregon	Five
Idaho	Nine	Pennsylvania	Nine
Illinois	Ten	Puerto Rico	Twelve
Indiana	Nine	Rhode Island	Three
Iowa	Seven	South Carolina	Six
Kansas	Four	South Dakota	Four
Kentucky	Seven	Tennessee	Three
Louisiana	Six	Texas	Two
Maine	Ten	Utah	Five
Maryland	Five	Vermont	Ten
Massachusetts	Five	Virginia	Four
Michigan	Three	Washington	Five
Minnesota	Four	West Virginia	Four
Mississippi	Four	Wisconsin	Ten
Missouri	Three	Wyoming	Three

Chapter Two

How To
Properly Prepare Your Purchase Agreements
And Protect Your Interests
When Buying Pre-Foreclosure Properties

Too many people falsely assume that a purchase agreement that's available for free on the Internet is perfectly legal in their state. It most likely isn't! That's because real estate contract law varies from state to state. I can't overemphasize the financial consequences that a poorly written purchase agreement can have, especially when put under the scrutiny of a judge, presiding over a lawsuit, filed by a disgruntled former homeowner, whose accusing you of "taking unfair advantage of their financial plight," while their loan was in foreclosure. And unlike conventional real estate transactions that are conducted between willing sellers and willing buyers, pre-foreclosure property sales, are almost always conducted between reluctant sellers, and overanxious buyers who are careless when it comes to preparing their purchase agreements. This combination of a reluctant seller and a buyer, who failed to properly prepare their purchase agreement, is a potential lawsuit waiting to happen. That's why when buying pre-foreclosure properties, you need to properly prepare your purchase agreements so that they:
1. Conform to your state's foreclosure and real estate sales statutes.
2. Are valid and legally enforceable in a court of competent jurisdiction.
3. Fully protect your position as buyer in a pre-foreclosure property transaction.

Twelve Key Provisions That Must Be Included In Your Purchase Agreements

The following twelve key provisions must be included in your purchase agreements, to clearly define the terms and conditions of the agreement, along with the rights and responsibilities of both the buyer and the seller:

1. **Parties to the agreement:** Designate all parties to the purchase agreement as buyer and seller to include their legal status as to whether they're a single individual, husband and wife or a business entity such as a corporation or limited liability company.
2. **Earnest money deposit:** State that if the buyer fails to perform this agreement within the time herein specified, the full amount of earnest money deposit made by the buyer shall be forfeited; however, such forfeiture shall jeopardize the seller's right to sue for specific performance.
3. **Legal description of property:** Use the exact same legal description that's written on the recorded deed of the property in the purchase agreement.
4. **Purchase price:** State the full purchase price of the property to include how the purchase is to be financed.
5. **Marketable title:** Specify that the seller is to furnish the buyer with an owner's title policy commitment letter insuring the marketability of the title to the property.
6. **Assignment of the purchase agreement:** Include a clause that the buyer has the right to assign or sell the purchase agreement to a third party.
7. **Default by buyer:** Specify that the earnest money paid is the sole and exclusive remedy in the event that the buyer fails to close on the purchase of the property.
8. **Default by seller:** State that the buyer shall have the right of specific performance in the event the seller defaults by refusing to sell the property.
9. **Eminent domain:** Specify that the buyer shall be entitled to a full refund of the earnest money deposit paid, plus any accrued interest, in the event the property is condemned by eminent domain prior to the closing date.
10. **Right of entry:** State that the buyer or buyer's assigns has the right, upon notifying the seller, to enter and inspect, repair, market and show the property to third parties prior to the closing date.
11. **Risk of loss:** Specify that the buyer is entitled to a full refund of the earnest money deposit paid, plus accrued interest, in the event the property is damaged or destroyed prior to the closing date.
12. **Right to examine all financial and tax records:** State that the buyer has the right to examine all of the financial and tax records associated with the property prior to the closing date.

Don't Use The Same Purchase Agreements That Real Estate Licensees Use

I highly recommend that you never use the same purchase agreements that are used by real estate licensees in your state, to purchase pre-foreclosure properties. That's because virtually all of the real estate agreements used by real estate licensees are written mainly to protect the licensees' sales commissions, and the legal rights and interests of the sellers who have listed their property through them. In addition to not being "buyer-friendly," these agreements are also not "investor-friendly" as they're geared towards traditional real estate transactions with conventional terms.

Hire An Experienced Board-Certified Real Estate Attorney In Good Standing

In order to avoid being bamboozled by some incompetent $300-an-hour attorney in an Armani suit and alligator shoes masquerading as a real estate attorney, I very highly recommend that you proceed with caution when selecting a real estate attorney to hire. You must hire an honest, competent, board-certified real estate attorney in good standing, who has experience with foreclosure actions in your state. Once hired, your attorney's job is to advise you on the proper preparation of your purchase agreement. A word of warning: please don't ignore the very sage advice that I'm dispensing here, and use the services of an attorney specializing in divorce law, to advise you on your state's foreclosure statute. If you expect to receive expert advice on real estate law, you must hire the services of an experienced, board-certified real estate attorney in good standing, who:

1. Specializes in the daily practice of real estate law.
2. Is well versed on how the foreclosure process works in your state.
3. Has ample experience preparing real estate purchase agreements.
4. Is affiliated with a reputable title insurance underwriter.
5. Is licensed to sell title insurance in your state.

The Standard Qualifications For An Attorney To Be Certified In Real Estate Law

The basic qualifications for attorneys to be certified in real estate law are pretty standard nationwide. For example, the Florida Bar requires that every attorney certified in real estate law must have practiced law for at least five years, with forty percent or more of their time spent in the practice of real estate law during the three years immediately preceding their application for certification. In addition, attorneys applying for certification must have passed a peer review, completed forty-five hours of continuing legal education within the three years immediately preceding their application, and passed a written examination.

The Standard Definition Of An Attorney In Good Standing

In most states, an attorney in "good standing" is defined as: *"those persons licensed to practice law who have paid annual state bar association membership dues for the current year, and who are not retired, resigned, delinquent, inactive, or suspended members of the state bar association."*

How To Find A Board-Certified Real Estate Attorney In Your Area

The best way to find a qualified, board-certified real estate attorney in your area is to contact your local bar association's lawyer referral service or your state's bar association lawyer referral service. Once you have the names of board-certified real estate attorneys in your area, you'll need to do an online search of your state's bar association membership rolls to verify that they're licensed to practice law in your state, and to also check if they've been disciplined, or had their license revoked for misconduct.

Attorney Locator Services Online

The following three Web sites provide online attorney locator services that allow you to search for an attorney by specialty and location:
Martindale Hubbell Lawyer Locator
www.martindale.com/locator/home.html
Findlaw
www.findlaw.com/14firms
Lawyers
www.lawyers.com

Make Certain Your Purchase Agreement Doesn't Violate Your State's Statutes

When buying homes from homeowners whose mortgage or deed of trust loans are in default and facing foreclosure, you must make certain that your purchase agreement doesn't violate any provisions in your state's foreclosure and real estate sales contract statutes. For example, many states, most notable California, have home equity sales contract statutes which allow homeowners in default the right to rescind or cancel a home equity sale's contract, usually within five business days--excluding weekends and holidays--after the purchase agreement was signed. Such statutes were enacted by state legislatures, to give financially distressed homeowners, a respite from the high pressure buying tactics used by some pre-foreclosure property investors. The following sample purchase agreement is for instructional and informational purposes only. I highly recommend that you seek the assistance of a board-certified real estate attorney, who's licensed to practice law in your state, to help you prepare a purchase agreement, to use to buy properties from owners in foreclosure.

Sample Purchase Agreement

This agreement made this tenth day of August 2003, between David D. Jones, a single man, known hereinafter as the Buyer and Donald S. Reed, a single man, known hereinafter as the Seller.

Seller agrees to convey, transfer, assign, sell and deliver to Buyer all of Seller's rights, title and interest in and to the following property known as 7202 West Lyman Road, Tampa, Florida 33609 and legally described as: Lot 34, Block17 of the Elliot and Harrison Subdivision, according to map or plat thereof, as recorded in Plat Book 37, Page 79, of the public records of Hillsborough County, Florida.

Seller agrees to sell to Buyer and Buyer agrees to buy from Seller under the following terms:

Purchase Price……………………………………………………………………………………..$130,000

Deposit held in escrow by John B. Good, Attorney at Law, in the amount of…..……………….$ 1,000

Subject to that certain mortgage dated August 28, 1997, and executed by David D. Jones, a single man as mortgagor, to Bank of Florida, as mortgagee, in the original amount of one-hundred and twenty-five thousand dollars, $125,000, which mortgage was duly recorded in the office of the Clerk of the Circuit Court of Hillsborough County, State of Florida, in book 790346, on page 45905, of the public records of Hillsborough County, Florida.

Loan payments, late fees, penalties, legal fees and accrued interest in arrears……………….. $ 6,900

Balance to close transaction payable in United States currency by cashier's check drawn on a local bank, subject to prorations or adjustments………………………………………………………. $ 5,900

Any net differences between the approximate balance of the existing encumbrance shown above and the actual balance at closing to include all unpaid loan payments, accrued interest, late charges, legal fees, taxes, liens, judgments, assessments, and fines shall be adjusted to the purchase price at closing.

In the event that all or any portion of the property shall be damaged or destroyed by fire or other casualty before closing, Buyer shall have the right to terminate this purchase agreement by providing Seller with a termination notice and will be entitled to an immediate refund of the deposit.

Buyer shall pay no consideration for the assignment of any escrow-impound funds held by the lender.

Title to the property shall be conveyed from Seller to Buyer by warranty deed at the closing.

This purchase is contingent upon Buyer's approval of the property's title and loan status.

Seller shall vacate the Property on or before August 28, 2002.

Buyer may assign Buyer's rights, title and interest in and to this purchase agreement to a third party.

The closing of this transaction shall take place at the office of attorney John B. Good, 4409 Himes Avenue, Tampa, Florida 33679 on or before August 28, 2003.

Seller accepts the foregoing offer and agrees to sell the herein described property to Buyer for the purchase price and on the terms and conditions herein specified.

All provisions of this Agreement shall extend to, bind, and inure to the benefit of heirs, executors, personal representatives, successors, and assigns of Seller and Buyer.

Seller and Buyer or Buyer's assigns, authorize Mr. John B. Good, Attorney at Law, to act as Escrow Agent and hold the earnest money deposit and close this transaction in accordance with the terms of this Agreement.

IN WITNESS WHEREOF, Seller and Buyer have set their hands the date aforesaid.

David D. Jones	Donald S. Reed
Seller	Buyer
Robert B. Big	Sally M. Little
Witness	Witness

Equity Purchase Agreement Notices Required By California Civil Codes

California Civil Codes require that the following notices be included in all equity purchase agreements on owner-occupied homes in foreclosure:

NOTICE REQUIRED BY CALIFORNIA LAW

Until your right to cancel this contract has ended, (Name) or anyone working for (Name), CANNOT ask you to sign or have you sign any deed or any other document.

The contract required by this section shall survive delivery of any instrument of conveyance of the residence in foreclosure, and shall have no effect on persons other than the parties to the contract.

You may cancel this contract for the sale of your house without any penalty or obligation at any time before (Date and time of day).

NOTICE OF CANCELLATION
(Enter date contract signed)

You may cancel this contract for the sale of your house, without any penalty or obligation, at any time before (Enter date and time of day).

To cancel this transaction, personally deliver a signed and dated copy of this cancellation notice, or send a telegram to (Name of purchaser), at (Street address of purchaser's place of business).

NOT LATER THAN (Enter date and time of day).

I hereby cancel this transaction (Date).

(Seller's signature)

Make Certain All Of Your Purchase Agreements Are Properly Witnessed

The reason why you must make certain the signatures on a purchase agreement are properly witnessed, is because documents that aren't properly witnessed, aren't in what's known as a "recordable form." This means that the document can't be recorded in the official public records. Each state has their own requirement as to the number of witnesses that are needed to attest the signatures on documents affecting real property. For example, in Florida, two witnesses are required to attest the signatures on real property title transfer documents.

Most Title And Escrow Companies Aren't "Investor-Friendly"

My idea of an "investor-friendly" title or escrow company is a company that's staffed with knowledgeable professionals who are ready, willing and able to do whatever it takes, within legal and ethical bounds, to close any type of real estate transaction. And, I can tell you that from my own personal experiences, I've found that most title and escrow companies aren't exactly what I'd call "investor-friendly." That's probably because most title insurance and escrow companies are generally leery of doing business with anyone they perceive as being "unconventional." By the very nature of their business, title and escrow companies are generally suspicious of any type of real estate transaction that involves more than a typical, run-of-the-mill, easy-to-close residential sale, with a buyer and seller, and two real estate agents. The average title or escrow agent doesn't understand how unconventional transactions are structured. And like most people, they fear what they fail to understand. This "fear factor" that most title and escrow companies seem to have about "real estate investors," fosters an atmosphere of mistrust that's not conducive to a good working relationship.

Best To Use A Board-Certified Real Estate Attorney To Close All Transactions

Instead of using title or escrow companies as closing agents, I recommend that you follow my advice, and hire an honest, competent board-certified real estate attorney to act as your legal counsel and closing agent in all real estate transactions. This way, you'll have someone working for you who:
1. Has a working knowledge of real property statutory regulations and case law.
2. Is experienced in solving complex legal problems related to real property.
3. Understands the mechanics of how judgments, liens and foreclosure actions work.
4. Has a fiduciary obligation to act in their client's best interest.

Ten Questions To Ask Owners In Foreclosure Before You Buy Their Property

Prior to buying any pre-foreclosure property, make certain that you have the property owner answer and sign a property disclosure statement, in the presence of a notary public, that asks the following ten questions:
Question #1: Are there any hazardous substances at, on, under or about the property? The term hazardous substances shall mean and include those elements or compounds which are contained in the list of hazardous substances and toxic pollutants adopted by the United States Environmental Protection agency or under any hazardous substance laws.
Question #2: Have any documents ever been filed in the public records that adversely affect the title to the property?
Question #3: Are there any liens against the property for unpaid bills owed to architects, surveyors, engineers, mechanics, laborers and materialmen?

Question #4: Are there any actions, proceedings, judgments, bankruptcies, liens or executions recorded among the public records, or pending in the courts, that would affect the title to the property?
Question #5: Are there any unpaid taxes or claims of lien, or other matters that could constitute a lien or encumbrance against the property or any of the improvements on it?
Question #6: Have any improvements been placed on the property in violation of applicable building codes and zoning regulations?
Question #7: Are there ongoing legal disputes concerning the location of the boundary lines of the property?
Question #8: Is any person or entity other than the owner presently entitled to the right to possession, or is in possession of the property?
Question #9: Has the title or ownership of the property ever been disputed in a court of law?
Question #10: Are there any unrecorded mortgage or deed of trust loans and promissory notes, for which the property has been pledged as collateral?

Prorate The Property Taxes Using The Three Hundred Sixty-Five Day Method

The three hundred sixty-five day method of proration is based on the assumption that every year has 365 days. For example, if the annual property tax bill for a pre-foreclosure property is $2,200, and the seller owned the property for 270 days, the seller's prorated portion of the tax would be $1,627.40 ($2,200 ÷ 365 days = $6.027 per day x 270 days = $1,627.40). However, if the property taxes for the current year can't be ascertained, stipulate in the closing statement that any tax proration based on an estimate shall be readjusted upon receipt of the tax bill.

Have All Utility Meters Read On The Day Before Closing

On the day before the closing, have all of the meters read by the public and private utility companies providing services that the property owner is responsible for paying. You must notify utility service providers that the property is under new ownership so that you don't get billed for utility services that were provided to the previous owner.

Double-Check All Closing, Loan And Title Transfer Documents For Mistakes

Don't automatically assume that the information contained in closing, loan and property title transfer documents is accurate and up-to-date. You must take the time to double-check all documents associated with the transaction for:
1. Mistakes made in computing prorations,
2. Mistakes made in transposing numbers and letters.
3. Mistakes made in spelling and typing.

Do A Final Walk-Around Inspection Of The Property On The Day Of The Closing

On the day of the closing, do a final walk-around inspection of the property to double-check for any last minute changes that may have occurred to the property that could have an adverse effect on its value. Use the property inspection checklist on the following page to conduct a final walk-around inspection of the property on the day of the closing:

Sample Walk-Around Property Inspection Checklist

1. Are there any condemnation notices posted on the property? ( ) Yes ( ) No
2. Are there bodies of standing water on the property that can't drain? ( ) Yes ( ) No
3. Are there any visible signs that the property is infested with termites or rodents? ( ) Yes ( ) No
4. Are there any visible signs of environmental hazards on the property? ( ) Yes ( ) No
5. Are there any code violation notices posted on the property? ( ) Yes ( ) No

Use A Closing Checklist To Catch Potential Problems Before The Sale Closes

I'm a firm believer in using a closing checklist like the sample copy below to catch potential problems before the sale closes and it's too late. Using a checklist approach helps to avoid overlooking any aspect of the property title transfer that could result in costly mistakes that aren't uncovered until there's a problem--usually many years later--and after the seller is long gone!

Sample Buyer's Closing Checklist

1. Review the title insurance policy.
2. Review the survey of the property.
3. Verify the property's legal description.
4. Verify the property's zoning designation.
5. Check with government agencies for building, fire, safety and health code violations.
6. Review the hazard insurance policy.
8. Review the termite inspection report.
9. Verify the property's tax payment status.
10. Compute the mortgage interest pro-ration.
11. Compute the real property tax pro-ration.
12. Check with government agencies for environmental hazard citations.
13. Review the bill of sale for personal property.
14. Review the deed.
15. Review the promissory note.
16. Review the mortgage.
17. Review the loan assumption documents.
18. Review the closing statement.
19. Verify that a current certificate of occupancy has been issued for the property.
20. Check with government agencies for municipal liens.

How To Avoid Getting Ripped-Off When Buying A Pre-Foreclosure Property

Lastly, in order to avoid being ripped-off by dishonest property owners in foreclosure, you must:
1. Not pay the lender to reinstate the loan in foreclosure until you've closed on the purchase of the property in foreclosure.
2. Not payoff any liens held by subordinate lienholders until you close on the purchase of the property in foreclosure.
3. Not pay the property owner for their equity until they have removed all of their possessions from the property and grounds.
4. Personally send the payment necessary to reinstate the loan directly to the lender via courier service.

Chapter Three

How To Use Foreclosure Notices To Find Property Owners Whose Loans Are In Default And Facing Foreclosure

When a lender declares a loan to be in default, the lender or the company servicing the loan directs their attorney or trustee to initiate a judicial or nonjudicial foreclosure action. The attorney or trustee then files a foreclosure lawsuit and notice of lis pendens, or a notice of default with the public or county recorder's office in the same county where the deed to the property being foreclosed on is recorded. And once a notice of lis pendens or a notice of default is recorded in the public records, it becomes what's known as public information. Foreclosure lawsuits and notices of default generally contain the:

1. Date the lawsuit or notice was recorded in the public records.
2. Names and addresses of defendant--mortgagor or trustor--whose loan is in default.
3. Names and addresses of the plaintiff--lender, trustee or beneficiary--foreclosing on the loan.
4. Case or notice of default number.
5. Property's street address.
6. Property's legal description.
7. Property's land use or zoning code.
8. Property's tax assessed value.
9. Original loan amount.
10. Date original loan was made.
11. Date last payment was made.
12. Amount of payments in arrears.
13. Loan balance at the time the foreclosure notice was filed.
14. Scheduled public foreclosure auction or trustee's sale date.

Difference Between A Delinquent Loan And A Loan That's In Default

The difference between a delinquent loan and a loan that's in default is as follows:
1. Delinquent loan. Most lenders consider any loan with payments that are thirty to eighty-nine days past due to be delinquent. And when a loan becomes delinquent, lenders send borrowers a loan breach letter like the sample copy below.
2. Loan in default. Most lenders consider any loan with payments that are ninety days or more past due to be in default.

Sample Loan Breach Letter

May 15, 2003

John J. Default
3345 Costa Rosa Way
Tampa, FL 33649

Re: Loan Number: FL08281950

Dear Mr. Default:

You have fallen behind on your mortgage payments. You must bring the mortgage current within thirty days of the date of this letter by sending the amount shown below to the Bank of Florida in the form of a money order or certified check.

The total amount due as of June 1, 2003 is $ 3,478.98.

To bring your account current, you must also include with the above payment, any payments or late charges that are due during this thirty-day period. Acceptance of less than the total amount due includes, but is not limited to, the principal and interest and all other outstanding charges and costs. Acceptance of less than the total amount due does not waive our right to demand the entire balance due under the terms of your mortgage agreement.

If you do not bring your loan current within thirty days from the date of this letter, the Bank of Florida will demand the entire balance outstanding under the terms of your mortgage agreement. This amount includes, but is not limited to, the principal and interest and all other outstanding charges and costs. The Bank of Florida will start legal action to foreclose on the mortgage, which will result in the sale of the property. We may also have the right to seek a judgment against you for any deficiency after the home is sold.

You have the right to bring your loan current after legal action has begun. You also have the right to assert in the foreclosure proceedings the nonexistence of the default or any other defense to our legal action and sale of the property.

We want to work with you to resolve the problem and help you bring your account into good standing. We urge you to contact Sally M. Little (813) 123-4567. Ms. Little will work with you to try to solve your current difficulty.

Sincerely,
William Z. Banker
Vice President

What You Need To Know About Notices Of Lis Pendens And Notices Of Default

In judicial foreclosure actions, lenders file a lawsuit to foreclose and a notice of lis pendens. A notice of lis pendens, like the sample copy listed below, is a legal notice, that's recorded in the public records, to give the public constructive notice, that a lawsuit affecting a property's title has been filed in a state or federal court of competent jurisdiction. In nonjudicial foreclosure actions, lenders file a notice of default. A notice of default, like the sample copy on the following page, is a legal notice that's recorded in the public record to give the public constructive notice that a mortgage or deed of trust loan is in default and scheduled to be foreclosed on.

Sample Notice Of Lis Pendens

IN THE CIRCUIT COURT OF THE THIRTEENTH JUDICIAL CIRCUIT
IN AND FOR HILLSBOROUGH COUNTY, STATE OF FLORIDA
CIVIL DIVISION

CITICORP MORTGAGE COPORATION

Plaintiff

vs.

CASE NO. 2003-782
DIVISION "B"

RAYMOND RYON,
BARNES INDUSTRIAL PIPING, INC.,
ALLEN DEVELOPMENT, INC.,
And UNITED STATES OF AMERICA,
Department of the Treasury-Internal Revenue Service

Defendants
_____/

NOTICE OF LIS PENDENS

TO: RAYMOND RYON,
     BARNES INDUSTRIAL PIPING, INC.,
     ALLEN DEVELOPMENT, INC.
     And UNITED STATES OF AMERICA,
     Department of the Treasury-Internal Revenue Service

YOU ARE NOTIFIED of the institution of this action, by Plaintiff against you seeking to foreclose a mortgage on the following property in Hillsborough County, Florida:

Lot 54, Block 18, Hyde Park, as per map or plat thereof as recorded in Plat Book 24 on Page 42 of the Public Records of Hillsborough County, Florida.

DATED THIS ninth day of July 2003.

Robert B. Big, Esquire
1950 Langdon Avenue, Suite 15
Tampa, FL 33629
Florida Bar Number 12345
(813) 123-4567

Sample Notice Of Default

IMPORTANT NOTICE

IF YOUR PROPERTY IS IN FORECLOSURE BECAUSE YOU ARE BEHIND IN YOUR PAYMENTS, IT MAY BE SOLD WITHOUT ANY COURT ACTION, and you may have the legal right to bring your account in good standing by paying all of your past due payments plus permitted costs and expenses within the time permitted by law for reinstatement of your account, which is normally five business days prior to the date set for the sale of your property. No sale date may be set until three months from the date this notice of default may be recorded (which date of recordation appears on this notice).

This amount is $4,567.89 as of May 1, 2003 and will increase until your account becomes current. While your property is in foreclosure, you still must pay other obligations (such as insurance and taxes) required by your note and deed of trust or mortgage. If you fail to make future payments on the loan, pay taxes on the property, provide insurance on the property, or pay other obligations as required in the note and deed of trust or mortgage, the beneficiary or mortgagee may insist that you do so in order to reinstate your account in good standing. In addition, the beneficiary or mortgagee may require as a condition to reinstatement that you provide reliable written evidence that you paid all senior liens, property taxes, and hazard insurance premiums.

Upon your written request, the beneficiary or mortgagee will give you a written itemization of the entire amount you must pay. You may not have to pay the entire unpaid portion of your account, even though full payment was demanded, but you must pay all amounts in default at the time payment is made. However, you and your beneficiary or mortgagee may mutually agree in writing prior to the time the notice of sale is posted (which may not be earlier than the end of the three-month period stated above) to, among other things, (1) provide additional time in which to cure the default by transfer of the property or otherwise; or (2) establish a schedule of payments in order to cure your default; or both (1) and (2).

Following the expiration of the time period referred to in the first paragraph of this notice, unless the obligation being foreclosed upon or a separate written agreement between you and your creditor permits a longer period, you have only the legal right to stop the sale of your property by paying the entire amount demanded by your creditor.

To find out the amount you must pay, or to arrange for payment to stop the foreclosure, or if your property is in foreclosure for any other reason, contact:

> XYZ Trustee Corporation
> 3745 Palmer Avenue
> Glendale, CA 91201
> (818) 123-4567

If you have any questions, you should contact a lawyer or the governmental agency, which may have insured your loan.

Notwithstanding the fact that your property is in foreclosure, you may offer your property for sale, provided the sale is concluded prior to the conclusion of the foreclosure.

REMEMBER, YOU MAY LOSE LEGAL RIGHTS IF YOU DO NOT TAKE PROMPT ACTION.

Foreclosure Notices Are Filed In The County Where The Property Is Located

To get copies of foreclosure notices--notices of lis pendens or notice of default--contact your county or public recorder's office, which may also go by any one of a number of other names such as the clerk of the county and circuit court, the county clerk's office, the circuit court clerk's office, the county registrar's office, or the bureau of conveyances. Whatever the name, all notices of foreclosure actions are filed, recorded and maintained at the recorder's office in your county.

Nationwide County Recorder Office Information Available Online

The Web site below has a listing of all of the county recorder offices nationwide:
National Recorders Directory
www.zanatec.com

Legal Notices Are Required To Be Published In A "Newspaper Of Record"

In order to give the public constructive notice about a foreclosure action, most state foreclosure statutes require lenders to publish legal foreclosure notices in a newspaper that's circulated within the same county where the foreclosure notice is recorded. In most counties, the county and circuit courts usually require that foreclosure notices be published in newspapers the courts have approved as "newspapers of record." A "newspaper of record," is a paper that has countywide circulation and is read by the majority of residents within the county. Call your county or public recorder to obtain the names of the newspapers of record for your county.

Where To Find Court And Commercial Newspapers

The Web site listed below has direct links to court and commercial newspapers nationwide:
American Court And Commercial Newspapers
www.primetimenewspapers.com/dcr/links.htm

In Many Counties Recorded Foreclosure Notices Can Be Accessed Online

Depending upon your state's public records statute, and whether or not your county's public records are available online, you should be able to access information on recorded notices of lis pendens and notices of default directly from your county or public recorder's records library. For example, here in Tampa, I can log onto the Hillsborough County Clerk of the Circuit Court Web site at www.hillsclerk.com, and click on the Online Records Search icon that goes to the Official Records Index Search Menu, where I can do a document search, by calendar date, for recorded notices of lis pendens. As an example, on August 28, 2003, I did a document search for all of the notices of lis pendens that had been recorded in Hillsborough County on August 22, 2003, as this was the most recent date that recorded documents were made available online. My search returned a listing of seventy-four notices of lis pendens for various types of civil lawsuits affecting the titles of real property. I can usually tell whether or not a notice of lis pendens is for a foreclosure action, by looking at the parties listed in the notice. For example, if one of the parties is a bank or mortgage lender, and the other party is a private individual or two people with the same last name, there's a pretty good chance that it's a mortgage foreclosure lawsuit. Once I've printed out the listing of notices of lis pendens, I then log onto the Hillsborough County Property Appraiser Web site at www.hcpafl.org, and do a property records search using the owner's name that's listed in the notice of lis pendens. And if I'm interested in the property after I've completed my property records search, I then send the property owner a copy of letter number one that's in chapter four. I've included a partial listing of the notices of lis pendens from my August 28, 2003 search, at the end of this chapter.

Most Foreclosure Reporting Services Provide Information Online

Most all foreclosure reporting services now provide foreclosure notices online. I highly recommend that you subscribe to an online foreclosure reporting service if there's one available in your area. Subscription rates vary depending upon the number of foreclosure filings listed and the frequency of publication. When selecting a foreclosure reporting service, pay special attention to how frequently--daily, twice-week, weekly, bi-weekly, or monthly--the report will provide you listings of foreclosure filings. You want to be certain you will be receiving current or fresh leads and not stale information that is weeks old and outdated. The following is a listing of Web sites that provide foreclosure notice information online:

RealtyTrac
www.realtytrac.com
Foreclosure Access
www.foreclosureaccess.com
PropertyTrac
www.propertytrac.com
Foreclosure Data NW
www.foreclosuredatanw.com
Information Resource Service
www.irsfl.com
New York Foreclosures
www.newyorkforeclosures.com
REDLOC
www.redloc.com
ForeclosureTrac
www.foreclosuretrac.com
Bates Foreclosure Report
www.brucebates.com
Foreclosure Reporting Service
www.foreclosure-report.com
Foreclosure Report
www.foreclosurereport.com
Real Data Corp
www.real-data.com
Midwest Foreclosures
www.midwestforeclosures.com
Foreclosure Listing Service
www.foreclosehouston.com
Foreclosure Disclosure Weekly
www.foreclosuredisclosure.com
County Records Research
www.countyrecordsresearch.com

Use Worksheets To Maintain Information On Foreclosure Notices

Use the following two worksheets to keep information on foreclosure lawsuits and notices of default:

Sample Foreclosure Lawsuit Worksheet

Property's street address_____
Tax assessor's parcel or folio number_____
Tax assessed value $_____ Date of last assessment_____
Foreclosure lawsuit case number_____ Date filed_____
Defendant/borrower's name_____ Telephone number_____
Defendant's address_____
Plaintiff/lender's name_____ Telephone number_____
Plaintiff's address_____
Plaintiff's attorney_____ Telephone number_____
Attorney's address_____
Scheduled foreclosure auction sale date_____ Minimum bid $_____
Type of loan in default: ( ) FHA ( ) DVA ( ) Conventional ( ) Private
Original loan date_____ Original loan amount $_____
Interest rate_____ Assumable?_____
Monthly loan payment: Principal $_____ Interest $_____
Taxes $_____ Insurance $_____ Total payment $_____
Unpaid principal loan balance $_____ Total loan payments in arrears $_____
Total amount of interest, late charges and legal fees owed $_____
Total amount needed to cure the default and reinstate the loan $_____

Sample Notice Of Default Worksheet

Property's street address_____
Tax assessor's parcel or folio number_____
Tax assessed value $_____ Date of last assessment_____
Notice of default case number_____ Date filed_____
Trustor's name_____ Telephone number_____
Trustor's address_____
Beneficiary's name_____ Telephone number_____
Beneficiary's address_____
Beneficiary's attorney or trustee_____ Telephone number_____
Trustee's address_____
Scheduled trustee auction sale date_____ Minimum bid $_____
Type of loan in default: ( ) FHA ( ) DVA ( ) Conventional ( ) Private
Original loan date_____ Original loan amount $_____
Interest rate_____ Assumable?_____
Monthly loan payment: Principal $_____ Interest $_____
Taxes $_____ Insurance $_____ Total payment $_____
Unpaid principal loan balance $_____ Total loan payments in arrears $_____
Total amount of interest, late charges and legal fees owed $_____
Total amount needed to cure the default and reinstate the loan $_____

Clerk of the Circuit Court
Hillsborough County, Florida

Official Records Index Results from Document Search by Date

Document: LIS PENDENS **Name:** **Recording Date:** 08222003

08/22/2003 **Verified Date** Available search dates are: January 1, 1965 to August 22, 2003

Message area: The query returned 74 records.

To Order Documents Online, recorded from 01/01/1990 thru 08/22/2003, click on the underlined Instrument Number.

Party Name	Cross Name	Rec Date	Document	Book	Page	Instr Num	Legal Desc
ALWAYS GREEN INC	DEUTSCHE BANK TRUST CO AMERICAS TRU	08/22/2003	LIS PENDENS	13004	1613	2003345750	L 10 B 2 WYNDHAM LKS PH 2
AMERICAS WHOLESALE LENDER	PERRONE DENNIS P	08/22/2003	LIS PENDENS	13004	1617	2003345753	L 21-24 B 22 RIO VISTA
ASKEW RONNIE LAMONT	HOME EQUITY ASSET TRUST 2002 4	08/22/2003	LIS PENDENS	13003	2	2003344938	L 6 B 5 CTRY PL #1
BA MORTGAGE LLC	GRIFFITH DENISE L LEBLANC	08/22/2003	LIS PENDENS	13004	1172	2003345666	L 2 B P BAYSIDE KEY PH II
BADCOCK W S CORP	OPTION ONE MORTGAGE LOAN TRUST 2001 B	08/22/2003	LIS PENDENS	13003	17	2003344943	PT S32 T32 R21
BANK OF AMERICA IL TRU	BENJAMIN MYRTLE DUNBAR	08/22/2003	LIS PENDENS	13004	1767	2003345793	L 12 B 41 REV MACFARLNES ADD W TPA
BANK OF AMERICA NA	GRIFFITH DENISE L LEBLANC	08/22/2003	LIS PENDENS	13004	1172	2003345666	L 2 B P BAYSIDE KEY PH II
BANK UNITED	MCINTOSH MICHAEL J SR	08/22/2003	LIS PENDENS	13003	44	2003344947	L 3 B 1 CRYSTAL COVE
BANKERS TRUST CO TRU	HALL CRAIG	08/22/2003	LIS PENDENS	13004	1613	2003345750	L 10 B 2 WYNDHAM LKS PH 2
BANKERS TRUST CO TRU	GRANT JACOB L	08/22/2003	LIS PENDENS	13004	1351	2003345699	L 34 MADISON TERR
BAYSIDE KEY HOMEOWNERS ASSN INC	BANK OF AMERICA NA	08/22/2003	LIS PENDENS	13004	1172	2003345666	L 2 B P BAYSIDE KEY PH II

Chapter Four

How To Contact Property Owners Whose Loans Are In Default And Facing Foreclosure

Most would-be pre-foreclosure property investors are under the misconception, that weary property owners, whose mortgage or deed of trust loans are in default and facing foreclosure, will welcome their "offer to help," with open arms. Believe me, nothing could be further from the truth! Fact is most owners in foreclosure, are usually in a very strong state of denial, and not exactly in the mood for casual conversations with complete strangers, spouting insincere gibberish about, "I'm here to help you!" So, how do you go about contacting property owners whose loans are in default and facing foreclosure? There are three methods you can use to contact owners in foreclosure, two of which I don't recommend. You can:
1. Do what I recommend and send letters or postcards to the address of the owner of record, that's listed in the county property appraiser or assessor's property records.
2. Do what I don't recommend and cold-call in person, at the address of the property, that's listed in the foreclosure lawsuit and notice of lis pendens, or notice of default.
3. Do what I don't recommend and cold-call by telephone, to the owner of record, at a telephone number that's listed in their name.

Best To Use Direct Mail To Contact Owners In Foreclosure

As far as I'm concerned, when properly used, direct mail is the quickest and most efficient method available for contacting all of the property owners in your county, whose mortgage or deed of trust loans are in default and facing foreclosure. A well organized and professionally run direct mail system, will enable you to make contact with defaulting property owners as soon as notices of their loan default are filed with the public or county recorder's office and become public information.

Furthermore, by mailing follow-up letters at regular intervals, every ten to fifteen days, you'll be able to maintain contact with owners in default, during their loan's reinstatement period, which is usually up to five days before the scheduled public foreclosure auction or trustee's sale date. However, in order to effectively and profitably use direct mail, you must get property owners whose loans are in default and facing foreclosure to:
1. Open your letters.
2. Meet with you face-to-face.
3. Negotiate with you.
4. Sell the equity in their property to you at a discount.

Most Letters To Owners In Foreclosure Are Very Poorly Written

The fact of the matter is, that most letters to property owners in foreclosure are very poorly written, and that's the main reason why direct mail doesn't work very well for most people. For example, every once and awhile, I'll read a very poorly written post on an Internet message board, where someone is whining about the lack of response they're receiving from the letters or postcards they're mailing to owners in foreclosure. How would you respond to "an offer to help," that was written on a sixth grade level? I don't know about you, but after I finished laughing, I would throw it in the trash. The point that I'm making here is that if you expect owners in foreclosure to take your letters or postcards seriously, they must be well written! Anything less is a waste of ink, paper, envelopes and stamps.

Why I Use Direct Mail To Contact Property Owners In Default

Here are four very good reasons why I use direct mail to contact property owners whose mortgage loans are in default and facing foreclosure:
1. **Direct mail is easy to use.** For example, all I have to do is sit at my computer, point and click and hit a couple of keys, and it'll print out any one of my six different letters to property owners in foreclosure. Once printed, it just needs to be signed folded and inserted into an envelope. My computer's operating system is Microsoft's Windows 2000 Professional that comes with the Microsoft Word 2000 program that can merge names and addresses with letters. I use window envelopes so I don't have to fiddle around addressing them.
2. **Direct mail is relatively cheap to use.** Direct mail gives me the most, bang, for my buck. For example, I can mail out one hundred letters first class mail, for right around $65. This includes the cost of letterheads, envelopes and postage, the whole shebang.
3. **Direct mail is quick.** I usually get responses from owners interested in selling within two weeks, from the date I mailed the letters out.
4. **Direct mail is effective.** It allows me to make direct contact with all of the property owners in my buying areas, whose mortgage loans are in default and facing foreclosure.

Send Letters To Owners In Default During The Loan's Reinstatement Period

The time to send letters to property owners whose loans are in default is during their loan's reinstatement period. The loan reinstatement period is the time period prior to the scheduled foreclosure or trustee's sale date. Loan reinstatement periods are given so that borrowers have an opportunity to cure their loan default by bringing their loan payments current to include payment of late charges, legal fees, and any additional costs incurred by the lender while the loan was in default. Borrowers in default on DVA, FHA, and Freddie Mac and Fannie Mae conventional loans have a borrower's right-to-reinstate clause in their loan documents that gives them the right to reinstate their loans up to five days prior to the foreclosure or trustee's sale taking place.

Hire A Professional To Write Your Letters

Who should write your letters to owners in foreclosure, depends upon how effective a writer you are. However, if you don't feel comfortable writing your own letters, I highly recommend that you hire a professional writer, who knows how to use the right words, that cause property owners in foreclosure to call you to set up a face-to-face meeting. You must hire a writer who knows how to write letters that appeal to the emotions of property owners facing foreclosure. After all, you need to get the owners to respond to your offer of immediate relief. Regardless of who writes your letters, they must be written, so that they focus totally on helping property owners solve their immediate problem of avoiding foreclosure and total loss of their equity. See the sample copies of the six different letters that I use to contact property owners in foreclosure, at the end of this chapter.

Letters Appealing To Emotions And Offering Immediate Relief Get Best Response

Property owners whose loans are in default and facing foreclosure usually act more on emotions such as fear, hostility and anxiety than on logic. Your letters should be written so that they:
1. Help to alleviate the property owner's anxiety and fear of the unknown.
2. Stress the benefits of selling now to include immediate cash for their equity and help in relocating.
3. Offer immediate relief from foreclosure, eviction and a blemished credit rating.

Mail Typewritten Letters That Are Individually Addressed And Personally Signed

One of your main objectives, when using direct mail, is to make each of your letters as personal as possible, in order to avoid the "mass mailing" look. Individually addressed and personally signed, typewritten letters, add a human touch, which gives them a much better chance of being opened and read, than impersonal, computer generated letters. Imagine the effect your envelope, would have, addressed to: "Dear Property Owner In Foreclosure" and your letter stamped with a signature stamp.

Send Your Letters Via First Class Mail

Sending your letters first class mail, avoids having them confused with bulk rate junk mail, that usually ends up unopened and in the trash. I recommend using first class stamps instead of metered mail. Also have **ADDRESS SERVICE REQUESTED** imprinted one quarter-of-an inch below your return address--which should consist of your typewritten and preprinted address, but not your name--so that the post office will give you the property owner's current address, if they have moved from the property. Furthermore, I recommend that you mail your letters on Wednesday or Thursday, so that property owners receive then on Saturday. It has been my experience that most property owners in foreclosure, seem to be more receptive to opening and reading their mail on the weekend, than during the rest of the week.

Send Multiple Follow Up Letters At Regular Intervals To Maintain Contact

Sending multiple follow up letters at regular intervals, every ten to fifteen days, to property owners facing foreclosure, greatly enhances your chances of getting a face-to-face meeting. To maximize your chances of this happening, you need to keep your name and telephone number in front of property owners, so that when they finally decide to sell their property, your name will be foremost on their minds. In most cases, when property owners finally decide they have to sell, they have very little time left and are forced to sell fast. If you send only one letter, that letter will most likely arrive before the owner has fully comprehended how little time they have and how precarious their position is. To be effective, one of your letters must arrive at the same time the property owner finally decides to sell. For example, in a state like California, which has a three-month loan reinstatement period, along with a twenty day trustee's sale advertising period, you may want to send a total of seven letters, one introductory letter and five follow up letters, mailed once every fifteen days, during the loan reinstatement period and one letter during the trustee sale advertising period. In states with shorter reinstatement time periods, you should send a follow up letter once every ten days. Each follow up letter should address the property owner's worsening plight--limited amount of time remaining to reinstate the loan and cure the default or sell the property--and your offer to quickly help them out of their situation, while there's still time left.

Use Postal Zip Codes To Target Potentially Profitable Properties

Rather than using the "shotgun" approach of mailing letters to every property owner in your county, whose loan is in default, I recommend you only mail letters to property owners in default, whose properties are located in desirable--stable, middle-income--neighborhoods, where properties are in demand. To be able to quickly determine which owners you should mail to, have the areas you want to buy in listed by their postal zip codes. Use the zip code directory available at your local post office, to obtain zip code information for your area. Using a zip code system, you can quickly check the property address on each foreclosure notice, against your listing of zip codes, to see if the property is located in a desirable area. Keep in mind that you may earn your profit when you buy, but you don't get paid until you sell. If you buy a pre-foreclosure property that you can't resell quickly, you won't make a profit, no matter how good of a buy you made. The key to quickly reselling your pre-foreclosure properties is to only buy properties in desirable areas.

Use Computer Files To Keep Track Of Your Letters To Owners In Default

I recommend that you create separate files in your computer's word processing program, to keep track of your letters to owners in foreclosure. For example, I use six separate letter files that are setup by date and zip code, to keep track of the six letters that I send to property owners in foreclosure in Hillsborough County, Florida. As an example, letter file number one is named 915.33629.1. The numbers 915 represents the day the letter was mailed, September 15, 2003. The numbers 33629 represents the zip code in Tampa, Florida, where I mailed the letters. The number 1 denotes that letter number one was mailed. This file contains the names and addresses of all of the property owners in the 33629 zip code that letter number one was mailed to, on September 15, 2003. This way, before letter number two is mailed out to the same property owners in the 33629 zip code, I can make all the necessary address changes or deletions, based upon the information that I've received from the property owners themselves, or the post office. I repeat this same procedure for letters number three through six. In the meantime, using newly recorded notices of lis pendens, I contact another group of property owners in foreclosure, using introductory letter number one, and repeat the same procedure for letters number two through six. All I have to do is change the date portion of letter file number one and rename it. To illustrate, the date on letter file number 915.33629.1, would be changed to 101.33629.1, for the first letters mailed on October 1, 2003 to property owners in zip code 33629.

Using Direct Mail To Contact Property Owners In Default Requires Persistence

Please keep in mind that the use of direct mail to contact property owners whose loans are in default and facing foreclosure is a number's game, requiring you to be consistently persistent. In order to be successful, you must mail introductory and follow-up letters to all the property owners in foreclosure, within your buying areas, on a regular basis. For example, you may initially mail out letters to two hundred property owners and only get responses from five of them. But if you bought one or two properties from the five property owners who did respond to your letters, and made a profit of $10,000 to $15,000 or more per deal, your efforts would have been very worthwhile. Use the sample property tracking worksheet below, to keep track of the pre-foreclosure properties that you're pursuing:

Sample Property Tracking Worksheet

Property's street address:_____
Property appraiser or assessor's folio or parcel number:_____
Tax assessed value $_____ Date of last assessment:_____
Owner's name:_____Telephone number:_____
Owner's address:_____
Date foreclosure lawsuit or notice of default recorded:_____
Foreclosure lawsuit or notice of default case number:_____
Scheduled foreclosure or trustee's sale date:_____
Final date to reinstate loan:_____
Date first letter mailed out:_____
Date second letter mailed out:_____
Date third letter mailed out:_____
Date fourth letter mailed out:_____
Date fifth letter mailed out:_____
Date sixth letter mailed out:_____
Date owner interviewed:_____

Why You Shouldn't "Cold-Call" In Person On Property Owners In Foreclosure

First off, put yourself into the shoes of a property owner in foreclosure and ask yourself this question: Would I be willing share my very personal financial plight with some unknown stranger banging on my front door? I hate to be a party-pooper, but cold-calling in person on property owners in foreclosure, has an extremely low success rate. Plus it's very time-consuming, and potentially very dangerous. I'm pretty certain that most of you are somewhat familiar with the term "road rage," well, go knocking on the door of a hostile property owner in foreclosure, and you just might experience a phenomenon known as "foreclosure rage!" That's because most people on the verge of losing their home and being put out on the street, don't act as rational, reasonable, intelligent adults. Rather, they're very angry people, who have no desire, to discuss their financial predicament, with someone whom they perceive, as being nothing more than a greedy opportunist, trying to profit from their misfortune. Please keep in mind that most people in foreclosure are scared, stressed-out and in a state of panic! However, if you fail to heed the sage advice that I'm dispensing here, and still want to cold call in person, on property owners in foreclosure, please be aware that you may be mistaken for a:
1. Lender's representative or a creditor and be verbally or physically assaulted.
2. Law enforcement officer or a bail bondsmen and be physically assaulted.
3. Prowler and be shot or stabbed.

4. Criminal attempting a home invasion robbery and be shot or stabbed.

What You Should Say When Cold-Calling On Owners In Foreclosure

Although I don't recommend it, but if you do cold-call on a property owner in foreclosure, please don't bang on the door and start the conversation off with some inane comment about "how you're there to help them!" All cold-call conversations with owners in foreclosure should be short, sweet and right to the point. Do not badger people, or try to pry into their business. Say your piece and then promptly leave if the homeowners don't respond to your offer to buy their house. The following dialogue, is an example, of how you should conduct a cold-call conversation:

Investor: Good evening Mr. And Mrs. Default. My name is Billy Buyer and I want to buy your house.
Homeowner: What makes you think that our house is for sale?
Investor: I've read in the public records that your loan is in default, and about to be foreclosed on.
Homeowner: Well it was, but that's been taken care of.
Investor: Good for you. While I'm here, I want to give you my business card, to let you know that I specialize in buying houses from people in foreclosure. Please don't hesitate to call me if I may ever be of assistance to you. It was nice meeting you. Good-bye.

Why Most Telephone Cold-Calls To Owners In Foreclosure Usually Don't Work

The main reason why most cold-calls to owners in foreclosure usually don't work is, because most of the people, who make cold-calls, are clueless about what they're actually going to say, if the owner answers the telephone. And as a result, what usually happens, on the very few occasions when the owner does answers their telephone, is that the caller either freezes up completely, or stammers through a poorly worded conversation, that's punctuated by long pauses and usually ends with the owner hanging up in disgust. So, if you do decide to cold-call an owner on the telephone, at the very least, know what you're going to say, before you make your call. Also, please be advised, that many owners in foreclosure:
1. Have unlisted telephone numbers.
2. Move out and abandon their property.
3. Refuse to answer their telephone.
4. Refuse to speak on the telephone with strangers about their financial problems.

Some Sage Advice about Dealing With Property Owners In Foreclosure

Lastly, over the years, I've had a lot of experience contacting property owners, who for whatever reason, have defaulted on their mortgage loans, and faced the very real prospect of foreclosure. And from my experiences, I've learned that most people in foreclosure:
1. Blame their financial plight on everyone, but themselves.
2. Are very reluctant to discuss their financial situation with strangers.
3. Are extremely hard to communicate with.
4. Very rarely tell the whole truth, at one time.
5. Are financially illiterate.
6. Have lousy credit and don't really care about their credit rating.
7. Are greedy and expect you to bail them out, and then pay them full retail value for their property.
8. Would rather have their loan foreclosed on, than sell their equity at a substantial discount, and allow, a "stranger," to profit from their misfortune.

Sample Letter Number One

Dear Mr. & Mrs. Debtor:

People have good reasons for missing mortgage payments!

No one wants to miss a mortgage payment. But oftentimes unexpected expenses crop up that just have to be met. You may have a health condition that needs attending or a family member who calls for your assistance.

Even banks know these things happen. And that is one reason why you can pay your monthly mortgage payment late--for a fee. So long as this happens only occasionally, there really isn't a problem. You're just out the extra fee.

The real problem begins when a property owner misses payment after payment. When this happens paying them back--getting back on schedule--becomes a major problem, especially if you've lost your job or have your income reduced for other reasons. Yes, then you have a real problem.

Each month in America, thousands of homeowners find that their situation has deteriorated to the point that their lender no longer feels that they'll be able to make their mortgage payments. And by then the lender initiates foreclosure action that begins a legal process that, if fully played out, enables the lender to sell the house at a public foreclosure auction sale.

Each year thousands of homeowners in Hillsborough County alone find themselves in this situation.

Fortunately, there are things you can do to protect yourself before this public foreclosure auction sale takes place and you are evicted from your house.

I know what they are and I'm in the business of helping you make the right choice at a difficult moment--a moment you probably feel more like burying your head in the sand.

However, behaving like an ostrich just is not very helpful--or smart.

Neither is letting your entirely understandable anxiety and, yes, embarrassment, dictate your decisions.

What makes sense is to understand the process that you're in, understand what you can do about it, and understand when it makes sense to take advantage of the service I can provide. I specialize in helping people who have defaulted on their mortgage payments and stand in danger of having their house sold at a public foreclosure auction sale by their mortgage lender and end up being evicted.

Pick up the phone right now and call me at (813) 237-6267. I will explain--without fee or obligation-- exactly what you need to do to solve your current problem. And I'll buy your house and give you a cashier's check within three days if you decide this makes the most sense for you.

I look forward to hearing from you soon, and to working with you to help solve your problem.

Sincerely,
<u>I mail this letter out as soon as the notice of lis pendens is filed with the clerk of the circuit court.</u>

Sample Letter Number Two

Dear Mr. & Mrs. Debtor:

Very, very soon the house you're living in could be taken away from you because you haven't made your mortgage payments.

Your mortgage lender has already filed a lawsuit in Hillsborough County Circuit Court to foreclose on your mortgage.

This means that if you can't bring your loan payments current before the suit becomes final, your house will be sold at a public foreclosure auction on the Hillsborough County Courthouse steps and you will be evicted. This is the law in Florida and if you fail to take action this will happen to you.

If your house is sold this way, you'll lose money. The average house sold at a public foreclosure auction sale in Hillsborough County sells for far less than its appraised value. That's money you need -- and that you'll not get. The bank holding your mortgage only cares about getting its money back. They don't care that you get yours, so the price they take is always much less than the current fair market value of your home. You lose.

To solve your problem, you could try to put your house on the market. Problem is that right now it currently takes about three months to sell a house in Hillsborough County.

What you need is money-- and you need it now.

Fortunately, I can help you get it.

I specialize in helping people just like you get out of the situation you are now in.

I'll buy your house and give you a cashier's check within three days--if you act now.

But you must act now!

Pick up the phone right now and call (813) 237-6267. I will explain--without fee or obligation -- exactly what you need to do to solve your current problem. And I'll buy your house and give you a cashier's check within three days if you decide this makes sense for you.

If you decide to sell, I'll even help you find another place to live-- free of charge.

I'll also help you in dealing with the title company handling the paperwork and deed transferring the property's title.

You can have a cashier's check in your hands within three days if you call me now at (813) 237-6267.

Sincerely,

__I mail this letter out approximately fourteen days after letter number one is mailed out.__

Sample Letter Number Three

Dear Mr. & Mrs. Debtor:

In less than two months, your house will be sold at a public foreclosure auction sale on the Hillsborough County Courthouse steps if you don't correct the problem you have with your mortgage lender.

You're now in the midst of a legal process that, if not solved, will result in your losing not only your house, but also all of your equity.

I last wrote to you two weeks ago so that this will not happen to you.

But you must act now!

Many people in your situation fall victim to their fears and anxieties and simply decide to do nothing.

They can't believe that their house can be repossessed and taken back from them by their bank. They can't believe the law allows this. And they hope that some angel will rescue them. They therefore hide inside their house, hoping the problem will simply go away, procrastinating about taking action. Meanwhile they are running out of time and options.

Do not let this happen to you.

Let me say again: the moment your mortgage lender filed a lawsuit to foreclose your mortgage, the law took over. If you take no action, your house can and will be sold right out from under you. The bank that loaned you the money to buy your house has the power to do this. And if you do not pay them what you owe them, they will.

You need money and you need it now. Why not schedule a free, no-obligation consultation meeting with me so I can discuss your options and, if this seems to be the best thing to do, sell your house. You can have a cashier's check within three days. A check that will enable you to end the legal hassle you are now facing.

I can help. But I need to see you! Call me now at (813) 237-6267 to schedule an appointment. You can have a cashier's check for your house within three days and put an end to the anxiety you are now going through.

Sincerely,

P.S. If you've already solved your cash problems and squared things with your lender, I would like to know so that I don't send you any more letters. But if you haven't solved your problems, why not let me help you?

<u>I mail this letter out approximately fourteen days after letter number two is mailed out.</u>

Sample Letter Number Four

Dear Mr. & Mrs. Debtor:

You have about six weeks--just six weeks-- remaining before your house is sold at public foreclosure auction on the Hillsborough County Courthouse steps.

You can stop the legal hassle.

Call me today for a free, no-obligation consultation on what you should do now. Your time really is running out. But I can give you a cashier's check for your house within ten days.

Call me at (813) 237-6267. I will get your mortgage lender off your back. And stop the stress and embarrassment of having your mortgage foreclosed on and you being evicted from your house. Also, I'll help you find a new place to live, and I'll give you a cashier's check for your house within three days!

Don't just sit back and do nothing. Act now while there's still time!

You know you need money. You know you need it now. So, act today to get it. Imagine. Just three days from today you can have a cashier's check from me and stop the legal hassle. Do it for your own piece of mind.

Sincerely yours,

P.S. If you've already solved your cash problems and squared things with your lender, I would like to know so that I don't send you any more letters. But if you haven't solved your problems, why not let me help you?

<u>I mail this letter out approximately fourteen days after letter number three is mailed out.</u>

Sample Letter Number Five

Dear Mr. & Mrs. Debtor:

You're running out of time to solve your problem.

Very, very soon you'll have nothing to say about what happens to your house. It will be sold at a public foreclosure auction sale on the Hillsborough County Courthouse steps.

Be honest with yourself for a minute. Do you really think your mortgage lender cares about what happens to you? They don't! They're really just interested in getting their money back.

What do you think? Houses sold at public foreclosure auction sales in Hillsborough County, usually sell for far less than their appraised value. But what does your mortgage lender care? They've got their money. You get whatever is left, which is usually nothing!

Is this what you really want?

Of course not!

And that is why you had better act now!

I can give you a cashier's check for your house within three days. That means you will get your mortgage lender off your back. And that you can stop the embarrassment and the hassle of what you are going through right now.

I can do all this--and help you find another place to live too.

All you have to do is call me right now at (813) 237-6267.

Time is not on your side in this one. If you do not take action now, your house will be auctioned off. And the Hillsborough County Sheriff's Department will evict you.

There is still enough time to make sure this does not happen to you.

My consultations are free and you have no obligation. Call me today at 237-6267 to protect your interests.

Very sincerely yours,

P.S. If you've already solved your cash problems and squared things with your lender, I would like to know so that I don't send you any more letters. But if you haven't solved your problems, why not let me help you?

<u>I mail this letter out approximately fourteen days after letter number four is mailed out.</u>

Sample Letter Number Six

Dear Mr. & Mrs. Debtor:

In less than two weeks, your house will be sold at a public foreclosure auction sale on the Hillsborough County Courthouse steps. Your mortgage lender will have one objective on that day: to get his money back out of your house. You'll have lost your house and your equity.

Are you prepared to lose your house and to be evicted-- all within the next two weeks?

I doubt it. This kind of experience is devastating to most people, numbing, bewildering, and painful.

You still have time--to save the situation. As I've been telling you the past several weeks, I can give you a cashier's check for your house within three days. I can stop the forced sale of your house. I can get your mortgage lender and their nagging representatives off your back. And I can help you find a new place to live.

The choice is up to you. To settle your affairs in a way that avoids any further embarrassment and confrontation, and ensures that you're treated fairly, and with dignity.

Or to let matters take their course -- and keep hoping for a miracle that is not going to happen.

Call me now. I can help you, just as I've helped other people in Hillsborough County. Even now, there's time to solve your problems to your advantage. But you must call me at today at (813) 237-6267.

This is my last letter to you. Shortly, you will be out of options and your house will be publicly auctioned off, and you will be evicted.

I wish you had let me help you avoid all of this. If you call me today, I still can. Please hurry.

Sincerely,

<u>I mail this letter out approximately fourteen days after letter number five is mailed out.</u>

Chapter Five

How To Perform Due Diligence On Pre-Foreclosure Properties

As I told you in the introduction of this book, one of the main reasons why most people fail to make it as pre-foreclosure property investors, is because they fail to perform thorough due diligence. And believe me, to be successful in this business you must have the most up-to-date and verifiable information that's available on a pre-foreclosure property and its owner. This way, you'll have all of the information that's necessary to make an informed, intelligent buying decision, that's based on "real time" information, and not outdated assumptions. Given today's computer technology, you can quickly perform most of your property due diligence research, simply by using your personal computer and an Internet connection, linking you to a myriad of Web sites, that'll enable you to quickly access the public records that are currently available online about a property's:

1. Ownership.
2. Liens.
3. Sales history.
4. Tax assessed value.
5. Neighborhood environmental hazards.
6. Neighborhood crime rate.
7. Neighborhood demographic and economic information.
8. Neighborhood real estate market conditions.

The Definition Of Due Diligence

In general legal terms, "due diligence," is defined as: *"The care that a reasonable, prudent person exercises in the examination and evaluation of risks affecting a business transaction."*

My Real Property Research Credo

Over the past twenty-three years, my real property research credo has evolved into: Trust no one, assume nothing, verify everything and be prepared for anything! I've learned the hard way not to automatically assume that all of the information contained in the official public records about a property is complete, up-to-date and one hundred percent accurate. It usually isn't. The only way to obtain reliable, up-to-date information is to go directly to the source of the information, and then verify it. For example, when I want to know the tax assessed value of a property, I first go online and lookup the property's street address on the Hillsborough County Tax Collector's Web site. I then call the tax collector's customer service department to verify that the property's tax account number and tax-assessed value that's shown on the Web site is accurate.

Perform Thorough Due Diligence Before You Make An Offer To Buy

The four main reasons for performing thorough due diligence on pre-foreclosure properties before you ever plunk down your hard-earned money, are to avoid:
1. Buying pre-foreclosure properties with "hidden" liens and other title problems.
2. Buying pre-foreclosure properties that are located in declining areas and extremely hard to sell.
3. Getting snookered into buying pre-foreclosure properties with "undisclosed" major defects and building code violations that are costly and time consuming to correct.
4. Buying pre-foreclosure properties contaminated with environmental hazards that can make the property uninhabitable, and render it worthless.

Use The Internet To Perform Due Diligence On Pre-Foreclosure Properties

As far as I'm concerned, the Internet is one of the greatest inventions of all time, and ranks right up there with flush toilets, sliced bread and basketball! And for real estate investors, the Internet is the single best property due diligence research tool available, especially for investors who are located in counties, where public records information is available online. If your county's property records are available online, you can quickly find out who owns a property, when it was purchased, how much it cost and its tax-assessed value. For example, here in Tampa, I can log onto the Hillsborough County Property Appraiser's Web site and armed only with a property's street address, I can almost instantly obtain the owner's name, mailing address, sale price and dates for the latest and prior sales, and the tax-assessed value of the property broken down by land and improvements. I can also get a site map plotting the improvements on the property, along with the tax account, or folio number assigned to the property. Then, I log onto the Hillsborough County Tax Collector's Web site, and type in the property's street address or tax folio number to obtain property tax information about the property's tax payment status.

Internet Search Engines

The following is a listing of the major Internet search engines:
Google
www.google.com
Lycos
www.lycos.com
Yahoo
www.yahoo.com

AltaVista
www.altavista.com
Vivisimo
www.vivisimo.com
Teoma
www.teoma.com
Excite
www.excite.com

Use A Checklist To Perform Due Diligence Research On Pre-Foreclosure Properties

I use the following checklist, to perform due diligence research on pre-foreclosure properties:
1. Property records search: Check your county property appraiser or assessor's property records for ownership information about the property.
2. Property tax records search: Check your county tax collector's property tax records for tax information about the property.
3. Comparable sales search: Check your county's property appraiser or assessor's records for recent sales of comparable properties within the same area during the past six months.
4. Neighborhood crime search: Check the crime risk rating for the property's address with local law enforcement agencies.
5. Flood zone map search: Check the property's address on local flood maps to determine if it's located in a flood zone.
6. Hazardous waste search: Check the property's address for environmental hazards with local, state and federal environmental protection agencies.
7. Demographic and economic data search: Check demographic and economic data for the property's address.
8. Code violation search: Check the property's address for code violations with your local code enforcement department.

Where To Find The Names Of All Of The Property Owners In Your County

The names of virtually every property owner in your county are available at your county property appraiser or assessor's office on what's known as the property tax roll. The property tax roll lists every parcel of land in a given county. Depending upon where you live, each parcel is assigned a separate tax identification number, either an assessor's parcel number, APN, or an appraiser's folio number.

Online Property Records Search

The following Web sites list the county property appraiser and assessor offices that have their property records available online:
Real Estate Public Records
www.real-estate-public-records.com
Search Systems
www.searchsystems.net
Tax Assessor Database
www.pubweb.acns.nwu.edu/~cap440/assess.html
Public Records Online
www.netronline.com/public_records.htm

National Association Of Counties
www.naco.org/counties/counties
Public Records USA
www.factfind.com/public.htm
✓ **International Association Of Assessing Officers**
www.iaao.org/1234.html
✓ **Public Records Research System**
www.brbpub.com

Six States Don't Require The Public Disclosure Of Real Estate Sales Information

In so-called nondisclosure states, only the principals and any real estate licensees involved in a real estate transaction know the sale price. The sale price of real estate transactions aren't publicly disclosed in the following six nondisclosure states:
1. Indiana.
2. Kansas.
3. Mississippi.
4. New Mexico.
5. Utah.
6. Wyoming.

Private Companies Maintain Real Property Ownership Records Databases

If you live in a nondisclosure state, you'll have to get sales data from a private company that maintains real property ownership records for your county, or from real estate licensees who have access to the local multiple listing service records. The following is a listing of Web sites of companies that maintain real property ownership record databases:
First American Real Estate Solutions
www.firstamres.com/html/home.asp
DataQuick
www.dataquick.com

What To Do If Your County's Property Records Aren't Available Online

If your county's property records aren't yet available online, contact your property appraiser or assessor's customer service department, to see if they provide property record information over the telephone. In most counties, you can call your property appraiser or assessor's customer service department, and give them a property's street address, and they'll be able to tell you the parcel or folio number, the owner's name and mailing address, if it's different than the property, when and how much the property last sold for, and the property's current tax-assessed value. This way, you won't have to trudge down to your property appraiser or assessor's office every time you want to lookup information.

Don't Be Bashful About Asking So-Called "Public Servants" For Help

I don't know about you, but I'm not the least bit bashful about asking the so-called "public servants" that staff government offices, for help! So the next time you visit your county recorder's office, explain to the people working in the public records library, that you're there to do a title search on a particular property, in order to uncover all of the encumbrances, such as mortgage or deeds of trust loans, along with any other liens and judgments, that are currently placed against the property's title. In most cases, they'll give you a brief orientation on how to locate a property's title information in the official record books, along with instructions on how to use their microfiche machines to read microfiche files.

How Parcels Of Land Are Identified For Tax Purposes

Most counties are divided up into map or plat books. Each map or plat book is given a separate number, and each parcel of land is given a separate tax identification number--an assessor's parcel number, APN, or an appraiser's folio number. The property appraiser or assessor assigns a folio number or assessor's parcel number to each parcel of land in the county. These assessor's parcel numbers or folio numbers, are used to compile the yearly property tax assessments, which are usually available online. They're also used to list each parcel owners' name, address, and the assessed value of both the parcel and any improvements. In some counties, lot and block numbers are used along with the subdivision's name.

How To Use Grantor And Grantee Indexes

When a deed is recorded in the public records, it is indexed in both a grantor--seller--index and, a grantee--buyer--index. Grantor and grantee indexes are maintained in alphabetical and chronological order. They're generally alphabetized according to last and first names. Let's assume that you're trying to determine a current property owner's name, but you have only the name of the person who last sold the property, and the year in which it was sold. To obtain the name of the current owner, you would use the grantor's index book, for the year the title was transferred, to locate the grantee's name. The grantor's index lists, in alphabetical order, all grantors named in documents recorded during a specific calendar year. And beside each grantor's name, is the name of the grantee as named in the document, along with the official record book and page number, where a photocopy of the recorded document can be located in the public records. The grantee index is arranged by grantee names, and gives the name of the grantee, and the official record book and page numbers, where a photocopy of the recorded document can be found.

How To Use A Tract Index

In some states, the grantor and grantee index system is supplemented, or has been totally replaced, by a tract index, which indexes all recorded deeds and liens by their location rather than by the property owner's name. In a tract index, one page is used for either a single parcel of land, or a group of parcels, called a tract, with all recorded deeds, mortgage and deed of trust loans, liens, judgments and other documents on the same page. The tract index system is much easier to use than the grantor and grantee system.

Many County Records Are Only Available On Microfiche Files

Prior to the advent of digital files, county or public recorder's offices used only a microfiche and microfilm index system to record and maintain property title documents. Once recorded, documents were placed directly onto microfilm, with each document being assigned a reel and frame number. If your county or public recorder's office hasn't made its records available online, microfilm readers are available in most courthouses so that the public may review microfiche files.

How To Locate The Owners Of Abandoned Properties In Foreclosure

Every once and awhile, you'll come across an abandoned property that's in foreclosure, and belongs to an owner who no longer resides at the post office mailing address that's listed on property title records. When this happens, go to the following sources in the county and state of the property's owner's last known address, and check the:
1. County voter registration records.
2. City and county public library patron records.
3. City and county business license records.
4. City and county jail inmate records.
5. State fishing and hunting license records.
6. State professional license records.
7. State department of motor vehicles.
8. State bar association membership records.
9. State vital statistics records.
10. State prison inmate records.
11. Federal prison inmate records.
12. Social Security Administration's Death Index.

Florida County Records Available Online

The Web site listed below has all of the Florida County public records that are currently available online:
Florida County Records Online
www.myfloridacounty.com

Documents Must Be Notarized And Recorded To Be Part Of The Public Record

All states require that any document, prior to its being recorded, first be acknowledged, that is witnessed and notarized, by a notary public. When recorded, property title documents are considered part of the public record, that is, information that's available to the general public. Recordation of property title documents, gives the public written notice of a party's interest, claim, and right to or in a specific property. This is known in legal terms as "constructive or legal notice," which means that anyone who needs to know is responsible for looking in the public records, to obtain knowledge of any and all parties claiming an interest or right to any property.

The Two Types Of Real Property Liens

Real property liens are legal claims, placed against a debtor's--lienee's--real property by lenders, creditors, and government agencies--lienors--to secure payment of a debt. The two types of real property liens are:
1. **Statutory liens.** Examples of statutory liens are mechanic's liens, state and federal income tax liens, and real property tax liens, which are created by statute.

✓ **2. Equitable liens.** Examples of equitable liens are mortgage and deeds of trust loans that are created by written agreements that pledge real property as security for a debt.

Specific Liens And General Liens

Real property liens are either:
1. **Specific liens.** Only attach to a debtor's specified piece of real property.
2. **General liens.** Sometimes referred to as name liens, which attach to all of a debtor's real and personal property located within the county where the lien was recorded.

A Liens Priority Is Determined By The Date Of Recordation And Type Of Lien

A lien's priority or seniority over other recorded liens placed against the title to the same property is determined by the date or chronological order in which it was recorded in the public records, and the type of lien. For example, a mortgage or deed of trust that was recorded on April 11, 2003, would have priority over another mortgage or deed of trust that was recorded on April 15, 2003, against the same property. That's because it would be in a first, or senior position over the second mortgage that was recorded against the property. However, in most states, property and special assessment tax liens to include liens placed against real property for unpaid governmental services have priority over previously recorded mortgage or deed of trust liens. Judgment liens, mechanic's liens, and even Internal Revenue Service tax liens don't have seniority over previously recorded mortgage or deed of trust liens, and are considered to be subordinate or junior liens.

Check The Public Records To Verify That All Recorded Liens Are Uncovered

Whatever you do, don't blindly rely on the lienholder information that's contained in foreclosure lawsuits and notices of lis pendens, and notices of default. When researching any pre-foreclosure property's title information, always make certain that you check the public records at the county recorder's library, to verify that all recorded liens placed against the property and owner, have been uncovered. <u>Check for both voluntary liens and involuntary liens.</u> Voluntary liens are liens that are placed against the title to real property with the owner's consent, such as mortgage or deed of trust loans. Involuntary liens are liens that are placed against the title to real property, as a result of legal action by a creditor, lender, or a government agency. However, functions of county and circuit court offices vary from state-to-state, sometimes even county-to-county. For this reason, I recommend that you contact your county courthouse, to find out exactly who, in your county, maintains records on real property and judgment liens. The following is a listing of where to look, and what to look for, when searching the public records for liens that are attached to property:

★ **1. County or public recorder's office.** Grantor and grantee or mortgagor and mortgagee indexes, federal tax lien index, old age assistance liens, conditional sales contracts (contracts for deed, agreements for deed, land sales contracts, etc.), notices of lis pendens index, writs of attachment (judgments), notices of foreclosure filings (foreclosure lawsuits and notices of default), mechanic's and materialmen's liens, and property tax liens.

2. Clerk of the county and circuit court. Defendant's judgment index, state income tax liens, state inheritance tax liens, state franchise tax liens, judgment liens, homeowner's association liens, suits to quiet title, suits for specific performance, suits to foreclosure, estates of deceased persons, guardianships of minors and incompetents, termination of life estates, termination of joint tenancies, and condemnation of lands.

3. United States Court. Federal judgments such as federal tax liens and judgment liens resulting from defaults on government guaranteed FHA, DVA, SBA and student loans.

4. Municipal clerk's records. Some liens result from unpaid bills for municipal services such as water and sewer services.

Fifteen Liens To Check For When Researching Pre-Foreclosure Property Titles

The following is a listing and brief description of the fifteen most common liens encumbering the titles to pre-foreclosure properties:

1. Real property tax liens. Real property tax liens are placed against properties by local taxing authorities--city and county tax collectors--when property owners fail to pay their property taxes. This results in the tax collector placing a tax lien against the property, in the amount of delinquent taxes owed, plus interest and penalties. If the tax lien is not paid, usually within a two to three year period after the first default, the tax collector then forecloses on the tax lien and sells the property at a tax deed sale. Check with the clerk of the circuit court, local tax collector's office, or county or public recorder's office.

2. Federal tax lien. In order for federal tax liens to attach to the titles of real property, the Internal Revenue Service, must file a Notice of Federal Tax Lien Under Internal Revenue Laws, Form 668, in the designated office of the county or state where the property subject to the lien is located. Or with the clerk of the United States district court for the judicial district, in which the property is located. If the Internal Revenue Service fails to properly file a federal tax lien, with the applicable office, the federal tax lien doesn't attach to the property's title. However, if a foreclosing lender fails to uncover a federal tax lien, which has been properly filed in the same county where the property being foreclosed on is located, the tax lien remains against the property's title. And the new owner would have to pay off the amount of the tax lien, plus interest and penalties in order to get it removed from the property's title. Check the federal tax lien file or index, in the county recorder's office or clerk of the circuit court.

3. Mechanic's lien. Mechanic's liens are statutory liens, which allow mechanics, contractors, materialmen, architects, surveyors, and engineers, who have furnished work or materials for the improvement of real property, to file a lien against the debtor's real property that's being worked on. The lien generally takes effect as of the date the labor or material was initially furnished. In most states, the lienor must show that the improvement was made at the request of the owner, or the owner's agent. Check with the county recorder's office or clerk of the circuit court.

4. Judgment liens. Judgment liens result from lawsuits awarding monetary damages. Once recorded, a lien is placed against both the real and personal property of the debtor, until the judgment is paid. Judgment liens usually only attach to property located in the county where the judgment was recorded. In most states, failure to voluntarily repay a judgment lien can result in the creditor getting the court to issue a writ of execution, allowing the county sheriff to seize and sell a sufficient amount of the debtor's property, to pay the debt and expenses of the sale. Note that judgments awarded by federal courts, usually against debtors, who default on federally guaranteed loans, such as Small Business Administration and student guaranteed loans, when recorded with the appropriate county clerk's office, attach to both the debtor's real and personal property. Check the defendant's judgment index at the clerk of the circuit court's office, or the county or public recorder's office.

5. Mortgage and deed of trust liens. A mortgage or deed of trust lien is a voluntary lien, that's created when real property, is pledged as security, for the repayment of a debt. If the debt secured by the mortgage or deed of trust lien, isn't repaid, the lender can foreclose on the security instrument-- mortgage or deed of trust--and sell the property at public foreclosure auction or trustee's sale. Check the grantor and grantee, or mortgagor and mortgagee indexes, at the county or public recorder's office.

6. **State inheritance tax liens.** Most states have an inheritance tax, which is levied against the estates of deceased persons. The amount of inheritance tax owed, becomes a lien against the estate. Check with the clerk of the circuit court or the county or public recorder's office.

7. **Corporate franchise tax liens.** States that have a corporate franchise tax, tax corporations for the right to do business within their state. When corporations fail to pay their franchise tax, the state files a lien against any real property, within the state that belongs to the corporation. Check with the clerk of the circuit court or the county or public recorder's office.

8. **Bail bond liens.** A lien is created when real property is pledged as a bail bond, in order to allow a person arrested on criminal charges, to be released on bail, pending trial. Check with the clerk of the circuit court or the county or public recorder's office.

9. **Code enforcement liens.** A lien is placed against a property's title, by local code enforcement boards, when a property owner, has been fined, for failing to correct code enforcement citations, and doesn't pay the fine. Check with the county or public recorder's office or the public recorder's office or the clerk of the circuit court.

10. **Municipal liens.** A lien is placed against a property's title by local governments, when a property owner fails to pay for municipal services such as water, sewage and trash removal. Check with the county or public recorder's office or the clerk of the circuit court.

11. **Welfare liens.** A lien is placed against a property's title, by state and federal government agencies, when a property owner, collects welfare payments that they're not legally entitled to. Check with the county or public recorder's office or the clerk of the circuit court.

12. **Public defender liens.** A lien is placed against a property's title, by federal, state and local governments, when a property owner, fails to pay for a court appointed public defender. Check with the county or public recorder's office or the clerk of the circuit court.

13. **Marital support liens.** A lien is placed against a property's title, by state and federal government agencies, when a property owner fails to pay court ordered marital support payments. Check with the county or public recorder's office or the clerk of the circuit court.

14. **Child support liens.** A lien is placed against a property's title, by state governments, when a property owner, fails to make court ordered child support payments. Check with the county or public recorder's office or the clerk of the circuit court.

15. **Homeowners' association liens.** A lien is placed against a property's title, by a homeowners' association, when an association member, fails to pay their homeowner's dues, as per the deed to their property. Check with the county or public recorder's office or the clerk of the circuit court.

How To Apply To Have A Federal Tax Lien Removed From A Property's Title

Internal Revenue Service publication number 783, is available at the Web page listed below, and has instructions on how to apply for a certificate of discharge of property from a federal tax lien.
Internal Revenue Service Publication 783
http://www.irs.gov/pub/irs-pdf/p783.pdf

Internal Revenue Service Office Location Nationwide

For a listing of Internal Revenue Service office locations nationwide, log onto the Web page listed below:
Internal Revenue Service Offices
http://www.irs.gov/localcontacts/#stateLinks

Where To Research Federal Bankruptcy Cases Online

Public Access to Court Electronic Records (PACER) is an electronic public access service that allows users to obtain case and docket information, from federal bankruptcy courts. Each federal bankruptcy district court, maintains its own case information. To learn more about PACER, log onto the Web site listed below:
PACER
www.pacer.psc.uscourts.gov/index.html

Most County Recorders Are Slow To Index Recorded Documents

For whatever reason, most county recorders are slow to index or place recorded documents into the public records. This can result in a recorded and valid lien not showing up during a lien search of the public records. I suggest that you ask the manager at your county or public recorders office, how long the time gap is between when a document is recorded and when it's actually indexed, into your county's public records. Because of this time gap, I recommend you check the lis pendens--lawsuits pending--index, at the clerk of the county and circuit court, or county recorder's office, for notices of any pending lawsuits, which may be filed against the title to the property. The names of the plaintiffs and defendants, in the lis pendens index, are arranged in alphabetical order.

Common Abbreviations Used In Property Title Documents

The following is a listing of abbreviations, commonly used in property title documents:
1. **Est.**--Estate
2. **Et al.**--And others
3. **Et vir.**--And husband
4. **Et ux.**--And wife
5. **Jt.**--Joint tenants
6. **Qc.**--Quit claim deed
7. **Lov**---Gift transfer
8. **Dot.**--Deed of Trust
9. **Grantor**-Seller
10. **Lt.**--Lot
11. **Com prop.**--Community property
12. **Ten in com.**--Tenants In Common
13. **Pcl.**--Parcel
14. **Tr.**--Trustee
15. **Sec.**--Section
16. **Blk**--Block
17. **Pt.**--Part
18. **Tr**--Tract
19. **Att.**--Attachment
20. **Ftl.**--Federal tax lien
21. **Jl.**--Judgment lien
22. **Ln.**-Lien
23. **Ml.**--Mechanics lien
24. **Stl.**--State tax lien
25. **Ttl.**--Town tax lien
26. **Cm.**--Committee deed
27. **Cn.**--Conservator deed
28. **Ex.**--Executor deed
29. **Gn.**--Guardian deed
30. **Mtg.**--Mortgage
31. **Pr Mtg.**--Prior mortgage
32. **Tcd.**--Tax collector deed
33. **Td.**--Trust deed
34. **Wd.**--Warranty deed

How Title Companies Index Documents In Their Property Records Databases

Unlike county and public recorders, who index recorded property title documents by name, title insurance companies index documents in their property records databases--title plants--by the legal description that's printed on the recorded document. The reason why title companies, index recorded documents by their legal description, is because it's faster and cheaper. The problem with indexing documents by their legal description is that documents containing erroneous legal descriptions end up being improperly indexed in the title company's database. For example, a valid mechanic's lien against Robert B. Big that contained an error in the legal description would not show up as a lien on a title search, that's done using the title company's database. However, the mechanic's lien would be found in a title search that was conducted using the name of Robert B. Big.

Best To Have Title Searches Done At The County Public Records Library

The official public records for every county, are located in the county or public recorder's records library. I recommend that you require your title searches, be conducted at the public records library in the county where the title to the property is recorded. The reason why I'm telling you to do this is because title company databases are indexed by legal descriptions, and not by the names of the parties, listed on recorded documents. This means that all of the valid liens recorded against a property's title, won't be discovered if a lien contains an incorrect legal description for the property

The Two Most Common Types Of Property Title Searches

The two most common types of property title searches are:
1. **Current owner and encumbrance (O&E) title search.** A current owner title search, sometimes referred to as an owner and encumbrance title or property report, is a search of the public records from the date the property's title was transferred to the current owner, to the present time.
2. **Full title search.** A full title search, involves an in-depth search of the property's chain of title, from the date the current owner took title, back to a maximum of <u>sixty</u> years.

Best To Hire An Experienced Title Abstractor To Perform Your Title Searches

Many investors have gotten into serious trouble, because they tried to save time and money, by doing only a cursory title search themselves, without having their search results, verified by an experienced title searcher or abstractor. That's because an uncovered, but recorded mechanic's lien, federal tax lien, or third mortgage or deed of trust loan, can come back to haunt you at a later date, usually when you're in the process of trying to resell the property. Researching property title information can sometimes be very tricky, even if you know what you're doing. That's why, I recommend, that you hire an experienced title abstractor, to do title searches, on pre-foreclosure properties that you're seriously interested in buying. To find an experienced title abstractor in your county, log onto the Web sites listed below:
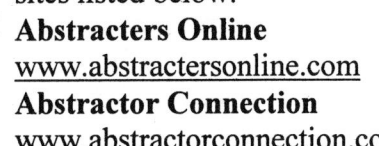 **Abstracters Online**
www.abstractersonline.com
Abstractor Connection
www.abstractorconnection.com

Online Crime Statistics Search

The following is a listing of Web sites that have nationwide crime statistics available online:
Crime.com
www.crime.com/info/crime_stats/crime_stats.html
Neighborhood crime check
www.apbnews.com/resourcecenter/datacenter/index.html

Online Demographic Information Search

The following is a listing of online sources of demographic information:
FFIEC Geocoding System
www.ffiec.gov/geocode/default.htm
U.S. Census Bureau FactFinder
www.factfinder.census.gov/servlet/BasicFactsServlet
U.S. Census Bureau Gazetteer
www.census.gov/cgi-bin/gazetteer
U.S. Census Bureau QuickFacts
www.quickfacts.census.gov/qfd/index.html
U.S. Census Bureau zip code statistics
www.census.gov/epcd/www/zipstats.html

Where To Search For People Online

The following Web sites provide people locator and street address information online:
Internet Address Finder
www.iaf.net
lookupusa
www.lookupusa.com
Switchboard
www.switchboard.com
Skipease
www.skipease.com
Social Security Administration Death Index
www.ancestry.com/search/rectype/vital/ssdi/main.htm
Street Address Information
www.melissadata.com/lookups/index.htm
Reverse Telephone Directory
www.reversephonedirectory.com

Verify The Property's Insurance Claims History Before You Make An Offer

Lastly, prior to making an offer to purchase a pre-foreclosure property, you must have your insurance agent or broker, verify the property's insurance claims history through the Comprehensive Loss Underwriting Exchange. The Comprehensive Loss Underwriting Exchange or C.L.U.E., is an insurance claim history information data exchange, that insurance companies use to calculate insurance premiums when underwriting policies. According to the Comprehensive Loss Underwriting Exchange Web site, their service: *"Provides loss history to help insurers qualify applicants and properties for homeowner coverage and helps insurers maximize premiums and minimize expenses."* You must do this to determine if the property is insurable, and if it can be insured at the prevailing market rate for similar properties within the same area.

Chapter Six

What You Need To Know About Real Estate Loans, Loan Covenants, Assumption Rules And Taking Title "Subject To" When Buying Pre-Foreclosure Properties

To be successful in this business, you must know as much about mortgage or deed of trust loans, loan covenants, assumption rules and taking title "subject to," as the lenders do that you'll be dealing with. You must know:
1. The names given to borrowers and lenders in mortgage or deed of trust loan documents.
2. The three loan covenants that pertain to loans in default.
3. The assumption rules for conventional and government insured and guaranteed loans.
4. Why taking title to a pre-foreclosure property "subject to" an existing loan can be risky business.

The Two Types Of Security Instruments Used To Secure Real Estate Loans

The two most common types of security instruments used to secure residential real estate loans are:
1. Mortgages.
2. Deeds of trust.

Mortgage Loans

The two parties to a mortgage are:
1. The mortgagor, (borrower).
2. The mortgagee, (lender).

When a real estate loan is secured by a mortgage, the mortgagor signs a promissory note and mortgage that the mortgagee keeps until the mortgagor pays the loan off.

Deed Of Trust Loans

The three parties to a deed of trust are:
1. The trustor, (borrower).
2. The beneficiary, (lender).
3. The trustee, (neutral third party holding the deed of trust).

When a real estate loan is secured by a deed of trust, the beneficiary makes a loan to the trustor and the trustor gives the beneficiary a promissory note and a deed of trust which conveys title to the trustee and is recorded and held in trust by the trustee until the loan is paid in full by the trustor.

The Two Different Types Of Lenders That Make Real Estate Loans

Most residential and commercial mortgage or deed of trust loans are made by the following two types of lenders:
1. Institutional lenders. Institutional lenders are: banks, credit unions, mortgage companies, mortgage bankers, commercial banks, pension funds and insurance companies that are licensed to make mortgage or deed of trust loans on residential and commercial real estate.
2. Private lenders. Private lenders are private individuals and privately held business entities that are licensed to make residential and commercial loans.

The Difference Between A Loan Broker And A Lender

The difference between a loan or mortgage broker and a lender is as follows:
1. Loan broker. A loan or mortgage broker is licensed to take loan applications from borrowers, and arrange loans between borrowers and lenders for a fee. Loan brokers are not licensed to make mortgage or deed of trust loans directly to borrowers.
2. Lenders. Lenders are licensed to make mortgage or deed of trust loans directly to borrowers.

Residential Mortgage And Deed Of Trust Loan Documents Are Available Online

You can download copies of the conventional residential mortgage or deed of trust loan documents that are used in your state from the following Web sites:
Fannie Mae Loan Documents
www.efanniemae.com/singlefamily/forms_guidelines/mortgage_documents/sec_instr.jhtml?role=ou
Freddie Mac Loan Documents
www.freddiemac.com/uniform

Loan Terminology Dictionary Available Online

The Web site listed below has a loan terminology dictionary:
Loan Terminology Dictionary
www.bcpl.net/~ibcnet/terms.html

Three Covenants That Pertain To Mortgage And Deed Of Trust Loans In Default

The three loan covenants contained in Fannie Mae and Freddie Mac conventional mortgage and deed of trust loan documents that pertain to loans in default are:

1. Transfer of the property or a beneficial interest in borrower. This covenant is the dreaded "due on sale clause" that allows lenders to call a loan if the title to the property securing the loan is transferred without the lender's prior approval.

2. Borrowers' right to reinstate after acceleration. This covenant gives the borrower whose loan is in default the right to cure the default and reinstate the loan by paying all loan payments, late fees and legal costs incurred by the lender while the loan was in default.

3. Acceleration remedies. This covenant gives lenders the right, upon default, to accelerate loan payments, and demand that the unpaid principle loan balance be paid in full within thirty days from receipt of notice.

Transfer Of The Property Or A Beneficial Interest In Borrower

This covenant is the dreaded "due on sale clause" that allows lenders to call a loan if the title to the property securing the loan is transferred without the lenders prior approval:

" As used in this Section 18, "Interest in the Property" means any legal or beneficial interest in the Property, including, but not limited to, those beneficial interests transferred in a bond for deed, contract for deed, installment sales contract or escrow agreement, the intent of which is the transfer of title by Borrower at a future date to a purchaser.

If all or any part of the Property or any Interest in the Property is sold or transferred (or if Borrower is not a natural person and a beneficial interest and a beneficial interest in Borrower is sold or transferred) without Lender's prior written consent, Lender may require immediate payment in full of all sums secured by this Security Instrument. However, this option shall not be exercised by Lender if such exercise is prohibited by Applicable Law.

If Lender exercises this option, Lender shall give Borrower notice of acceleration. The notice shall provide a period of not less than 30 days from the date the notice is given in accordance with Section 15 within which Borrower must pay all sums secured by this Security Instrument. If Borrower fails to pay these sums prior to the expiration of this period, Lender may invoke any remedies permitted by this Security Instrument without further notice or demand on Borrower."

Borrowers' Right To Reinstate After Acceleration

This covenant gives the borrower whose loan is in default the right to cure the default and reinstate the loan by paying all loan payments, late fees and legal costs incurred by the lender while the loan was in default. *"If Borrower meets certain conditions, Borrower shall have the right to have enforcement of this Security Instrument discontinued at any time prior to the earliest of: (a) five days before sale of the Property pursuant to any power of sale contained in this Security Instrument; (b) such other period as Applicable Law might specify for the termination of Borrower's right to reinstate; or (c) entry of a judgment enforcing this Security Instrument. Those conditions are that Borrower: (a) pays Lender all sums which then would be due under this Security Instrument and the Note as if no acceleration had occurred; (b) cures any default of any other covenants or agreements; (c) pays all expenses incurred in enforcing this Security Instrument, including, but not limited to, reasonable attorneys' fees, property inspection and valuation fees, and other fees incurred for the purpose of protecting Lender's interest in the Property and rights under this Security Instrument; and (d) takes such action as Lender may reasonably require to assure that Lender's interest in the Property and rights under this Security Instrument, and Borrower's obligation to pay the sums secured by this Security Instrument, shall continue unchanged. Lender may require that Borrower pay such reinstatement sums and expenses in one or more of the following forms, as selected by Lender: (a) cash; (b) money order; (c) certified check, bank check, treasurer's check or cashier's check, provided any such check is drawn upon an institution whose deposits are insured by a federal agency, instrumentality or entity; or (d) Electronic Funds Transfer. Upon reinstatement by Borrower, this Security Instrument and obligations secured hereby shall remain fully effective as if no acceleration had occurred. However, this right to reinstate shall not apply in the case of acceleration under Section 18."*

Acceleration Remedies

This is the acceleration covenant that gives lenders the right, upon default, to accelerate loan payments, and demand that the unpaid principle loan balance be paid in full within thirty days from receipt of notice: *"Lender shall give notice to Borrower prior to acceleration following Borrower's breach of any covenant or agreement in this Security Instrument (but not prior to acceleration under Section 18 unless Applicable Law provides otherwise). The notice shall specify; (a) the default; (b) the action required to cure the default; (c) a date, not less than 30 days from the date the notice is given to Borrower, by which the default must be cured; and (d) that failure to cure the default on or before the date specified in the notice may result in acceleration of the sums secured by this Security Instrument, foreclosure by judicial proceeding and sale of the Property. The notice shall further inform Borrower of the right to reinstate after acceleration and the right to assert in the foreclosure proceeding the non-existence of a default or any other defense of Borrower to acceleration and foreclosure. If the default is not cured on or before the date specified in the notice, Lender at its option may require immediate payment in full of all sums secured by this Security Instrument without further demand and may foreclose this Security Instrument by judicial proceeding. Lender shall be entitled to collect all expenses incurred in pursuing the remedies provided in this Section 22, including, but not limited to, reasonable attorneys' fees and costs of title evidence."*

The Due On Sale Clause As Defined In The Federal Code Of Regulations

Title Twelve, Volume Five, of the Code of Federal Regulations as of January 1, 2003, defines the due on sale clause as follows: *"Due-on-sale clause means a contract provision which authorizes the lender, at its option, to declare immediately due and payable sums secured by the lender's security instrument upon a sale of transfer of all or any part of the real property securing the loan without the lender's prior written consent. For purposes of this definition, a sale or transfer means the conveyance of real property of any right, title or interest therein, whether legal or equitable, whether voluntary or involuntary, by outright sale, deed, installment sale contract, land contract, contract for deed, leasehold interest with a term greater than three years, lease-option contract or any other method of conveyance of real property interests."*

Loan Assumption Rule For Federal Housing Administration Insured Loans

Federal Housing Administration (FHA), federally insured loans closed prior to December 14, 1989, can be assumed without qualification simply by paying an assumption fee, or taken "subject to" without paying any assumption fee. FHA insured loans closed after December 15, 1989, can only be assumed by qualified owner-occupants and contain a due-on-sale clause that "bans" investors from ever being able to assume them.

Loan Assumption Rule For Department Of Veterans Affairs Guaranteed Loans

Loans guaranteed by the Department of Veterans Affairs (DVA), which were closed prior to March 1, 1988, contain no due-on-sale clause and may be assumed by anyone without qualification by paying an assumption fee, or taken "subject to" without paying an assumption fee. DVA guaranteed loans originated on or after March 1, 1988, contain a due-on-sale clause requiring prior approval by the DVA or its authorized agent before any DVA guaranteed loan can be assumed. All DVA mortgage or deed of trust loans have the following statement printed on the top of the first page of the loan document **"THIS LOAN IS NOT ASSUMABLE WITHOUT THE APPROVAL OF THE DEPARTMENT OF VETERANS AFFAIRS OR ITS AUTHORIZED AGENT."**

Installment Sale Contracts Don't Violate The Due On Sale Clause In DVA Loans

Installment sale contracts such as contracts for deed (CFD) and agreements for deed (AFD), don't violate the due on sale clause contained in Department of Veterans Affairs (DVA) loans. Section 12 of DVA Circular 26-90-37, Dated September 25, 1990, reads as follows: *"Sale Agreements Not Subject to 38 U.S.C. 1814. When a borrower sells on an installment contract, contract for deed, or similar arrangement in which title is not transferred from the seller to the buyer, this is not considered a "disposition" of residential property securing a GI loan as stated in 38 U.S.C. 1814, and therefore does not require approval by VA or the loan holder prior to the execution of such an agreement. However, any borrower considering a sale in this manner should be cautioned that under such an arrangement he or she remains liable for repayment of the loan. Even if the agreement calls for the contract purchaser to make payments directly to the GI loan holder, the holder is not required by VA to change its records, and the contract seller is responsible for forwarding payment coupons and other information to the contract purchaser. Depending on the particular circumstances of a case, a holder may agree to change the account address to read in care of the contract purchaser, although the contract seller must promptly advise the holder of any change in his or her address."*

No Stated Loan Assumption Rules For Private And Seller Financed Loans

Private real estate loans made by private individuals, and purchase money first or second mortgage and deed of trust of loans made by sellers may or may not contain due-on-sale clauses. A word of caution: many private lenders may claim that their loan contains a due-on-sale clause when in fact it doesn't. Therefore, it's crucial that you personally read the entire mortgage or deed of trust along with the promissory note when reviewing any loan documents for due-on-sale clauses. This is especially true with private and purchase money loan documents, many of which are poorly written and don't contain a due-on-sale clause. This means that if the mortgage or deed of trust, or promissory note doesn't contain a due-on-sale clause, the lender can't call the loan, or stop a buyer from taking the property's title "subject to" the existing loan.

Personally Review All Loan Documents For Due-On-Sale Clauses

How do you know if a loan document or promissory note contains a legally enforceable due-on-sale clause? The best way is for you to personally review all loan documents--mortgages, deed of trust, and promissory notes--for due-on-sale clauses. Ask sellers to show you copies of both their mortgage or deed of trust and promissory note. Your goal in doing this is to determine whether or not the loan in default has a legally enforceable due-on-sale clause before you contact the lender.

Taking Title "Subject To" Violates The Due On Sale Clause In Most Loans

You need to know that taking title to a property "subject to" an existing residential mortgage or deed of trust loan is in direct violation of the due on sale clause that's contained in virtually all residential loan documents, used by institutional lenders. This means that when a lender discovers that a sale has taken place in violation of the loan's due on sale clause, the lender has the following three options:
1. Call the loan and exercise their right to accelerate payments and demand that the entire unpaid principle loan balance be paid in full within thirty days.
2. Foreclose on the loan if the new owner fails to pay it off after the lender calls the loan due.
3. Do nothing and let the new owner take over the loan payments.

Taking Title To Property "Subject To" Existing Loans Can Be Risky Business

Contrary to popular belief, almost all transactions that are made "subject to" existing loans are usually quickly discovered by lenders. The discovery almost always occurs, when the lender receives a hazard insurance policy that has the new owner's name as the insured, instead of the name of the borrower of record. As far as I'm concerned, buying pre-foreclosure properties "subject to" existing loans, without the prior approval of the lender, can be risky business. That's because in my professional opinion, there's a better than fifty percent chance, that the lender will call the loan after the sale takes place, and demand that the entire unpaid principal loan balance, be paid in full within thirty days. I say this because the loan is already under close scrutiny by the lender, because of its default status. In other words, the loan is on the lender's brightly flashing radar screen. For this reason, I recommend that if you do take title "subject to," an existing mortgage or deed of trust loan that's in default, that you don't invest a lot of money to cure the default and reinstate a loan. This way, if the lender does call the loan, and you aren't able to pay it off, you'll be able to keep your losses to a minimum.

It's Not A Criminal Act To Violate A Loan's Due On Sale Clause

In spite of the constant bullspit being espoused by a certain Harvard Business School graduate, posing as a "real estate savant," violating a loan's due-on-sale clause isn't against the law, nor is it a criminal act, punishable by imprisonment, or a monetary fine! It's a breach of a covenant contained in conventional and government-backed residential loan agreements that gives lenders the option to call a loan due. For example, if a borrower violates a loan's due on sale covenant, and it's discovered by the lender, the lender has the right to call the loan due and payable in full within thirty days. And if the borrower doesn't pay the loan off within thirty days, the lender has the right to declare the loan in default, and file a foreclosure lawsuit and notice of lis pendens, or a notice of default. Trust me, no member of any law enforcement agency that's allowed to operate within the borders of the United States, is going to haul you off to jail, just because you violated a loan's due on sale clause!

Ask The Lender To Modify The Loan Agreement So That It Can Be Assumed

If you're leery about the potential risk associated with taking title to a property "subject to" existing loans, you can do what I occasionally do, when I buy a property that I want to hold onto, and that is ask the lender to modify the loan agreement, so that you can formally assume the loan. In most cases, if you're creditworthy and have sufficient income, the lender will approve the loan assumption without changing the terms of the loan.

Notify The Lender That You Plan On Taking Title "Subject To" Their Loan

One surefire method of gauging how aggressive a lender is about enforcing the due on sale clause contained in their loans is to send a matter-of-fact letter to the president of the bank, informing the bank that you plan on taking title to a property "subject to" their loan! I've done this twice, and have never received a response from the lender. And both times, I went ahead and took title to the property "subject to" the existing mortgage loan. Fact is, if either lender had decided to try and call their loan due, months after the transaction was completed, my defense would've been, that I had put them on notice of my intentions, and they had failed to act in a timely manner. I don't know whether or not I would've prevailed in a court of competent jurisdiction, but I do think it would've been a viable defense, that wouldn't be laughed out of court.

The Difference Between Assuming An Existing Loan And Buying "Subject To"

When a buyer "assumes" an existing mortgage or deed of trust loan, they sign an assumption agreement with the lender that makes them legally responsible for repayment of the loan. When a buyer takes title to a property "subject to" the existing mortgage or deed of trust loan, all they're really doing is "taking over the loan payments" without accepting the responsibility for repaying the loan. That's because buying "subject to," totally eliminates the buyer from being held personally liable for repayment of the promissory note. The responsibility for repayment of the loan always lies with the last owner "assuming" the loan, prior to its being taken "subject to."

Include A "Subject To" Clause In Your Purchase Agreement

To take title "subject to" an existing mortgage or deed of trust loan, you must insert a "subject to" clause, similar to the one below in your purchase agreement:

Sample "Subject To" Clause

Subject to that certain mortgage dated August 28, 1997, and executed by David D. Jones, as mortgagor, to the Bank of Florida, as mortgagee, in the original amount of one-hundred and twenty-five thousand dollars, $125,000, which mortgage was duly recorded in the office of the Clerk of the Circuit Court of Hillsborough County, State of Florida, in book 790346, on page 45905, of the public records of Hillsborough County, Florida.

The Definition Of Equity Skimming

Equity skimming as it pertains to taking title "subject to" an existing mortgage or deed of trust loan that's in default is defined as: *"A pattern of conduct in which a buyer defrauds a property owner of their equity interest or other value in real property under the guise of a purchase of the owners' property, but which is in fact a device to convert the owners' equity interest or other value in real property to a buyer, who fails to make payments, diverts the equity or other value to the buyers' benefit, and leaves the property owner with a resulting financial loss or debt."*

What You Need To Know About Equity Skimming

First off, equity skimming is illegal in all fifty states of the United States of America. Secondly, equity skimming is a federal crime punishable by a fine of not more than $250,000 or imprisonment not more than five years, or both. Equity skimming occurs when a property owner uses any part of the rents, assets, proceeds, income or other funds derived from the property covered by a mortgage or deed of trust loan as personal funds. In a typical pre-foreclosure property equity skimming scam, a scam artist takes title "subject to" an existing mortgage or deed of trust loan that's in default for little or nothing down. The scam artist then either resells the property on a wraparound mortgage or all inclusive trust deed and collects loan payments, or rents it out and collects rental payments for months on end without ever making a single loan payment to the lender. This goes on until the lender finally forecloses on the loan and evicts the unsuspecting "owner" or tenant. In the meantime, the poor sap whose name is on the loan now has a foreclosure listed in their consumer credit file, and is more than likely on the hook for a deficiency judgment from the lender. Don't do it!

The Federal Equity Skimming Statute

Under Chapter 12, United States Code, Section 1709-2, equity skimming is defined as:
"Whoever, with intent to defraud, willfully engages in a pattern or practice of--
(1) purchasing one-to four-family dwellings (including condominiums and cooperatives) which are subject to a loan in default at time of purchase or in default within one year subsequent to the purchase and the loan is secured by a mortgage or deed of trust insured or held by the Secretary of Housing and Urban Development or guaranteed by the Department of Veterans Affairs, or the loan is made by the Department of Veterans Affairs,
(2) failing to make payments under the mortgage or deed of trust as the payments become due, regardless of whether the purchaser is obligated on the loan, and
(3) applying or authorizing the application of rents from such dwellings for his own use, shall be fined not more than $250,000 or imprisoned not more than 5 years, or both. This section shall apply to a purchaser of such a dwelling, or a beneficial owner under any business organization or trust purchasing such dwelling, or to an officer, director, or agent of any such purchaser. Nothing in this section shall apply to the purchaser of only one such dwelling."

Chapter Seven

How To
Quickly Verify Loan Information
With Foreclosing Lenders

Time is always of the essence when verifying loan information with foreclosing lenders. That's because most property owners whose loans are in default wait until the "eleventh hour"--usually less than ten days before their scheduled public foreclosure auction or trustee sale date--before they finally realize they won't be able to bring their loan payments current in order cure the default and reinstate the loan. They wait until the last moment before they finally decide they have no choice but to sell their equity in the property before the public foreclosure auction or trustee's sale takes place, and they end up with no more than an eviction notice. Prior to making an offer on any pre-foreclosure property, you need to verify a property's loan information directly with the foreclosing lender to determine:
1. The type of loan in default: DVA, FHA, conventional, or private.
2. The unpaid principle loan balance, interest rate, amortization period and total monthly payment to include principle, interest, taxes and insurance.
3. The total amount of loan payments, late charges, penalties and legal fees that must be paid in order to cure the default and reinstate the loan.

Verify All Loan Information Directly With The Foreclosing Lender

When doing a pre-foreclosure property analysis, please don't depend on any loan information, which may be published in foreclosure lawsuits, notices of lis pendens and notices of default. And, definitely don't depend on what the property owner in default may tell you. Make sure that you verify all loan information directly with the foreclosing lender. Verifying loan information directly from the foreclosing lender is absolutely crucial to determine if a particular pre-foreclosure property; has enough equity to make it worth pursuing.

Contact All Foreclosing Lenders Through The Property Owner In Default

Since all lenders require that all loan information requests be made in writing by the borrower--mortgagor or trustor--I suggest that you contact all lenders by going through the property owner whose mortgage or deed of trust loan is in default. Doing so will allow you to expedite the loan verification process and close the sale much faster. However, before contacting the foreclosing lender, compile as much loan information as you can upon your initial meeting with the owner. Review the owner's mortgage or deed of trust loan documents, promissory note, loan payment coupon book, and the latest yearly loan escrow analysis statement, which should have the loan's unpaid principle balance. Use a loan worksheet like the sample copy below to keep track of loan information:

Sample Loan Worksheet

First lender:_____
Loan account number:_____
Loan officer:_____ Telephone number:_____
Type of loan: ( ) FHA ( ) DVA ( ) Conventional ( ) Private
Original loan date:_____ Original loan amount $_____
Interest rate:_____ Assumable? ( ) Yes ( ) No
Monthly loan payment $_____
Unpaid principle loan balance $_____
Total amount of loan payments in arrears $_____
Total amount of accrued interest, late charges, penalties and legal fees owed $_____
Total amount needed to cure the default and reinstate the loan $_____
Second lender:_____
Loan account number:_____
Loan officer:_____ Telephone number:_____
Type of Loan: ( ) Conventional ( ) Private
Original loan date:_____ Original loan amount $_____
Interest rate:_____ Assumable? ( ) Yes ( ) No
Monthly loan payment $_____
Unpaid principle loan balance $_____
Total amount of loan payments in arrears $_____
Total amount of accrued interest, late charges, penalties and legal fees owed $_____
Total amount needed to cure the default and reinstate the loan $_____
Third lender:_____
Loan account number:_____
Loan officer:_____ Telephone number:_____
Type of Loan: ( ) Conventional ( ) Private
Original loan date:_____ Original loan amount $_____
Interest rate:_____ Assumable? ( ) Yes ( ) No
Monthly loan payment $ _____
Unpaid principle loan balance $_____
Total amount of loan payments in arrears $_____
Total amount of accrued interest, late charges, penalties and legal fees owed $_____
Total amount needed to cure the default and reinstate the loan $_____

Have The Owner Request An Estoppel Letter From The Foreclosing Lender

The only way to legitimately verify loan information from foreclosing lenders is for the lender to provide the owner in default with a mortgage or deed of trust estoppel letter verifying the type of loan, unpaid principle loan balance, interest rate, total monthly payment and the total amount needed to cure the default and reinstate the loan. "Estoppel" is a legal doctrine, which prevents parties from denying facts, which they have certified as being true. For example, if a lender sends you an estoppel letter stating that Mr. & Mrs. Default's mortgage or deed of trust loan has an outstanding principle loan balance of $52,750, at eight percent interest with a total monthly loan payment of $725 as of a specific date, the lender can't later claim that the loan balance was really $62,750. I recommend that you call the foreclosing lender to get the name of the person in charge of the mortgage or deed of trust loan loss mitigation department before you send your estoppel letter. This way, the owner in default will have the name of a real live person to call if you don't receive a quick response to your estoppel letter request. Then have the owner in default sign the estoppel letter so that you can send it via facsimile to the person in charge of the loan loss mitigation at the foreclosing lender's office. To request a mortgage or deed of trust estoppel letter from a foreclosing lender, send a letter like the sample copy below:

Sample Request For Mortgage Or Deed Of Trust Estoppel Letter

Dear Sir:

Reference mortgage loan number: 0124567890
Mortgagor: Robert S. Reed

Please send a facsimile of the following information regarding my mortgage loan to Mr. David D. Jones at (813) 123-4567:

Principle and interest payment $_____ Original loan amount $_____
Insurance payment $_____ Date of original loan:_____
Tax payment $_____ Payment due date:_____
Interest rate:_____ Escrow impound balance $_____
Total monthly payment $_____ Principle balance $_____
Total amount of loan payments in arrears $_____
Total amount of accrued interest, late charges, penalties and legal fees owed $_____
Total amount needed to cure the default and reinstate the loan $_____

Thank you in advance for your prompt attention to this matter.

Sincerely,

How To Negotiate With Private Lenders Holding Loans That Are In Default

When negotiating with private lenders holding mortgage or deed of trust loans that are in default, point out that if you take title to the property in foreclosure "subject to" their mortgage or deed of trust, you'll be saving them the expense of having to go through the entire foreclosure process. Plus, you'll save them the expense and hassle of trying to resell their property after the foreclosure auction or trustee's sale takes place. In addition, point out to private lenders that you'll be bringing all of the back loan payments current so that, in effect, the lender won't lose any money by letting you take over the loan. However, try to avoid paying any accrued interest and late charges or penalties to private lenders. In some cases, you may even be able to negotiate a discount on the loan payments in arrears. It always pays to ask. The worst the lender can say is no. However, be advised that private lenders holding loans on properties in areas with rapid appreciation may not be willing to let you take over or assume loans that are in default. In other words, in hot markets, private lenders will generally enforce due-on-sale clauses so they can get property back and resell it for a quick profit. Send private mortgage or deed of trust lenders a letter like the sample copy below when you find a property with a privately held mortgage or deed of trust loan that's in default and worth pursuing:

Sample Letter To Private Mortgage Or Deed Of Trust Lenders

Dear Mr. Martin,

My name is David D. Jones, and I'm interested in possibly purchasing the property at 6723 Vermont Avenue, Tampa, FL 33607, from Mr. Donald S. Reed, that you hold a first mortgage loan on.

Mr. Reed will call you this morning to give you authorization to release information to me regarding your first mortgage loan.

Mr. Reed has told me that the loan's unpaid principle loan balance is around $175,000 with an annual interest rate of nine percent, and that his monthly loan payments are approximately $8,700.00 in arrears.

As you may know, the property is currently in a neglected, run-down physical condition with numerous building code violations. As a result of the property's current condition, no institutional mortgage lender will make a loan against it. I estimate it will cost around $25,000 to correct the numerous code violations and bring the property into compliance.

Because of the current physical and financial condition of the property, I would be interested in possibly assuming Mr. Reed's existing first mortgage loan.

Once you have Mr. Reed's permission, please send me via facsimile at (813) 123-4567, the following information regarding the mortgage loan:
1. Principle unpaid loan balance $_____
2. Amount of loan payments, accrued interest, late charges and penalties in arrears $_____
3. Annual interest percentage rate:_____
4. Amortization period:_____
5. Prepayment penalty: ( ) Yes ( ) No
6. Monthly principle and interest payment $_____

Thank you for your cooperation in this matter.

I look forward to working with you to bring Mr. Reed's situation to a mutually beneficial solution.

Sincerely,

David D. Jones

Chapter Eight

How To Conduct A Thorough Property Inspection

Prior to ever making an offer to buy a pre-foreclosure property, have the property thoroughly inspected. You must do this in order to avoid being bamboozled by an unscrupulous owner surreptitiously masking a property's major defects. Who should inspect your property for major defects depends upon how much construction knowledge and experience you have. If you lack the necessary knowledge and experience, you should hire a retired tradesmen or professional property inspector to snoop around and inspect the property for major defects that some owners will try and hide. Conduct a search on the Internet to obtain the names of certified or licensed property inspectors in your area. If you know what you're doing, you can do your own property inspections. That's what I do when I need to have a property inspected. I simply make an appointment with the owner and show up at the property in my old coveralls with my high-powered searchlight, trusty ice pick, binoculars, extension ladder, mini-tape recorder and inspection checklists, and inspect the property for:

1. Structural roof damage.
2. Sinking and cracking foundations.
3. Mold contamination.
4. Electrical, fire and safety hazards.
5. Structural dry rot damage.
6. Water and moisture intrusion.
7. Collapsed water and sewer lines.
8. Signs of termite infestation.
9. Missing roofing material, gutters and downspouts.
10. Rotting wood.
11. Stripped mechanical systems and missing electrical wiring.

Inspect "Suspicious Properties" For Environmental Contamination

In order to avoid buying a potential toxic waste dump, have "suspicious properties" inspected for various types of environmental contamination that could make a property uninhabitable and render it worthless. By a "suspicious property," I mean a property that has been used to house businesses such as gas stations, dry cleaners, automobile repair shops and other businesses that use petroleum products, cleaning solvents and hazardous chemicals. Even if you don't suspect that a property has any type of environmental contamination, use the phase one environmental audit checklist below to conduct your own inspection.

Sample Phase One Environmental Audit Checklist

1. Examine the property's chain of ownership for the past fifty years.
2. Interview the current and available past owners of the property to determine if any present or past uses of the property would have an adverse affect upon the environment.
3. Review available past city cross-reference street directories to determine how the property was previously used.
4. Review available topographic maps of the property.
5. Review available historical aerial photographs of the property.
6. Review available geological reports affecting the property.
7. Research local, state and federal government files for records of environmental problems affecting the property.
8. Research local, state and federal government files for records of environmental problems affecting adjacent properties.
9. Conduct an on site inspection of the property for obvious signs of past or present environmental problems such as odors, soil staining, stress vegetation or evidence of dumping or burial.
10. Determine the existence and condition of above ground storage tanks.
11. Determine the existence and condition of underground storage tanks.

Online Environmental Hazardous Waste Search

To perform an online environmental hazardous waste search on a pre-foreclosure property, log onto the following Web sites:
EPA superfund hazardous waste site search
www.epa.gov/superfund/sites/query/basic.htm
Environmental hazards zip code search
www.scorecard.org
EPA Enviromapper zip code search
www.epa.gov/cgi-bin/enviro/em/empact/getZipCode.cgi?appl=empact&info=zipcode
HUD environmental maps
www.hud.gov/offices/cio/emaps/index.cfm

Housing Built Before 1978 May Pose Potential Lead-Based Paint Hazards

The Residential Lead-Based Paint Hazard Reduction Act requires that all sales agreements to sell residential property built before 1978 contain a Seller's Lead-Based Paint Disclosure Statement that discloses, whether or not the property has been inspected for lead-based paint hazards, and if lead-based paint hazards have been found on the property.

Online Lead-Based Paint Hazard Information

The following is a listing of online sources of lead-based paint hazard information:
EPA National Lead Information Center
www.epa.gov/lead/nlic.htm
Lead-Based Paint Disclosure Fact Sheet
www.epa.gov/opptintr/lead/fs-discl.pdf
Lessor's Lead-Based Paint Disclosure Statement
www.epa.gov/opptintr/lead/lesr_eng.pdf
HUD Lead-Based Paint Abatement Guidelines
www.lead-info.com/abatementguidelinesexamp.html
EPA Lead information Pamphlet
www.hud.gov/lea/leapame.pdf

Use HUD's *Minimum Property Standards For Housing* Handbook For Inspections

HUD Handbook, 4910.01 R01, *Minimum Property Standards For Housing*, is an excellent property inspection resource that can be ordered online from the HUD Direct Distribution System for free. To order your copy, log onto:
HUD Direct Distribution System
www.hud.gov/dds/index.cfm

How To Find A Competent Building Inspector

If you lack the construction knowledge and experience that's needed to conduct a thorough property inspection, you should hire a professional building inspector to snoop around and inspect properties for you. A word of caution: Be very careful when hiring a building inspector. The home and building inspection profession has more than its fair share of phonies, fakes, frauds and scam artists. That's because most states don't have any licensing requirements for home or building inspectors. For example, in Florida, anyone can become a "home inspector" simply by obtaining a city or county occupational business license. The best advice that I can give you is to use an inspector who's a member of the American Society of Home Inspectors. The American Society of Home Inspectors has very strict membership requirements. You can log onto the American Society of Home Inspectors' Web site listed below to find members who are located in your area.
American Society of Home Inspectors
ashi.org/find

Use Inspection Checklists To Conduct Your Pre-Buy Property Inspections

The following pages contain my pre-buy property inspection checklists. My inspection checklists are unique because they all contain a repair cost column. The reason I added this column was to allow the inspector to use the same form to do a rough repair cost estimate. My inspection forms allow for a fast but thorough inspection of any property.

Sample Exterior Property Checklist

Street address: _____

Item	Good	Fair	Bad	Repair Cost
Roof				
Foundation				
Siding				
Windows				
Doors				
Carport				
Garage				
Paint				
Screens				
Soffit & Fascia				
Chimney				
Steps				
Other				

Sample Grounds Inspection Checklist

Street address:_____

Item	Good	Fair	Bad	Repair Cost
Lawn				
Plants & Shrubs				
Trees				
Driveway				
Sidewalks				
Pot Holes				
Sink Holes				
Drainage				
Streets				
Outside Lighting				
Other				

Sample Attic Inspection Checklist

Street address:_____

Item	Good	Fair	Bad	Repair Cost
Ventilation				
Insulation				
Floor				
Lighting				
Roof Rafters				
Ceiling Joists				
Wiring				
Air Ducts				
Termite Damage				
Mold				
Other				

Sample Garage And Carport Inspection Checklist

Street address:_____

Item	Good	Fair	Bad	Repair Cost
Walls				
Floor				
Ceiling				
Doors				
Windows				
Lighting				
Heat				
Air Conditioning				
Paint				
Roof				
Soffit & Fascia				
Mold				
Other				

Sample Electrical Inspection Checklist

Street address:_____

Item	Good	Fair	Bad	Repair Cost
Riser				
Service Panel				
Capacity				
Circuit Breakers				
Electrical Outlets				
Lighting				
Wiring				
Electrical Meter				
Other				

Sample Plumbing Inspection Checklist

Street address:_____

Item	Good	Fair	Bad	Repair Cost
Water Supply				
Hot Water Heater				
Toilets				
Sinks				
Tub				
Shower				
Septic System				
Water Pipes				
Drains & Sewer Lines				
Water Pressure				
Plumbing Fixtures				
Water Supply Lines				
Well				
Mold				
Other				

Sample Heating And Air Conditioning Inspection Checklist

Street address:_____

Item	Good	Fair	Bad	Repair Cost
Natural Gas				
Central Heat & Air				
Oil Furnace				
Window & Wall Units				
Solar Panels				
Vents				
Condenser Unit				
Heat Pump				
Mold				
Other				

Sample Kitchen Inspection Checklist

Street address:_____

Item	Good	Fair	Bad	Repair Cost
Floor				
Walls				
Ceiling				
Doors				
Windows				
Lighting				
Electrical Outlets				
Sink				
Plumbing				
Cabinets				
Countertops				
Refrigerator				
Oven				
Ceramic Tile				
Paint				
Mold				
Other				

Sample Bathroom Inspection Checklist

Street address:_____

Item	Good	Fair	Bad	Repair Cost
Floor				
Walls				
Ceiling				
Doors				
Windows				
Lighting				
Electrical Outlets				
Shower				
Tub				
Ceramic Tile				
Sink & Vanity				
Ventilation				
Linen Closet				
Mirrors				
Paint				
Mold				
Other				

Sample Dining Room Inspection Checklist

Street address:_____

Item	Good	Fair	Bad	Repair Cost
Floor				
Walls				
Ceiling				
Doors				
Windows				
Lighting				
Electrical Outlets				
Paint				
Carpet				
Mold				
Other				

Sample Living Room Inspection Checklist

Street address:_____

Item	Good	Fair	Bad	Repair Cost
Floor				
Walls				
Ceiling				
Doors				
Windows				
Lighting				
Electrical Outlets				
Paint				
Carpet				
Mold				
Other				

Sample Bedroom Inspection Checklist

Street address:_____

Item	Good	Fair	Bad	Repair Cost
Floors				
Walls				
Ceilings				
Windows				
Doors				
Lighting				
Electrical Outlets				
Closets				
Carpet				
Paint				
Mold				
Other				

Sample Home Office Inspection Checklist

Street address:_____

Item	Good	Fair	Bad	Repair Cost
Floors				
Walls				
Ceilings				
Windows				
Doors				
Lighting				
Electrical Outlets				
Storage Closets				
Carpet				
Paint				
Mold				
Other				

Chapter Nine

How To Accurately Estimate The Current Market Value Of A Pre-Foreclosure Property

One of the worst mistakes that any pre-foreclosure property investor can ever make, is to pay too much for a property. That's because for many investors, overestimating the value of a property usually proves to be a very costly and fatal mistake that generally marks the beginning of the end, of their foray into buying pre-foreclosure property. That's why it's imperative that you learn how to accurately estimate the current market value of a pre-foreclosure property. As far as I'm concerned, it's the single most important aspect of the entire pre-foreclosure property buying process! And just what exactly does the term "current market value" mean? It means the value of the property in its current financial and physical condition, after deducting all of the costs associated with curing the default and reinstating the loan and paying off all of the recorded liens and judgments, and repairing the property to a marketable resale condition. In order to accurately estimate a pre-foreclosure property's current market value, you must first know the:

1. Principle loan balance of the mortgage or deed of trust loan that's in default.
2. Total amount of loan payments in arrears.
3. Total amount of accrued interest, late charges, penalties and legal fees that are owed.
4. Total amount needed to cure the default and reinstate the loan.
5. Total amount of all of the liens and judgments that are recorded against the property's title.
6. Total cost of all repairs needed to put the property in a marketable resale condition.
7. Cost of buying the seller's equity at a minimum discount of fifty percent.
8. Property's market value, based on the sales data of comparable properties, that have sold within the same area, during the past six months.

No Kelly Blue Book For Real Estate Investors To Lookup Used Property Values In

Because there's no **Kelly Blue Book** equivalent for real estate investors to lookup used property prices in, you're going to have to learn for yourself, how to accurately estimate the current market value of pre-foreclosure properties. However, thanks to computers and the Internet, in most real estate markets, it's not that difficult to get an accurate estimate of a property's current market value. This is especially true for real estate investors located in counties, where all property ownership, sale and tax assessment records are readily available online.

The Definition Of Market Value

The Appraisal Foundation's **Uniform Standards of Professional Appraisal Practice,** defines "market value," as: *"the most probable price a property should bring in a competitive and open market under all conditions requisite to a fair sale, the buyer and seller each acting prudently and knowledgeably, and assuming the sale price isn't affected by undue stimulus."* This definition assumes that the following conditions are met:
1. The buyer and seller are motivated.
2. Each party is well informed and acting in their own best interests.
3. A reasonable amount of time is allowed for the property to be exposed on the open market.
4. Payment is made in cash in U.S. dollars or in comparable financial arrangement.
5. The price represents the normal consideration of the property sold, and is unaffected by special or creative financing or sales concessions granted by anyone associated with the sale.

The Difference Between A Property's Assessed Value And Its Appraised Value

The difference between a property's tax-assessed value and its appraised value is as follows:
1. **Tax assessed value:** Tax-assessed value is the value established by the local taxing authority for a parcel of land and the improvements placed upon the land, for property tax purposes. For example, in Florida, owner-occupied single-family houses are generally assessed at around seventy percent of their fair market value by county property appraisers.
2. **Appraised value:** Appraised value is the value estimate given to a property by a licensed property appraiser, using accepted appraisal methods for the type of property being appraised. For example, the accepted appraisal method to accurately estimate the fair market value for an owner-occupied single-family house is the comparison sales method where a property's value is based on the recent sale of comparable properties within the same area.

Most Owners Of Residential Properties In Foreclosure Have No Equity

I hate to be the bearer of bad news, but you need to know, that most of the residential properties in foreclosure, aren't worth pursuing. That's because, prior to defaulting on their first mortgage or deed of trust loan, most of the owners in foreclosure, refinanced their loans, in order to suck all of the equity out of their property. This lack of equity in residential properties in foreclosure, is a direct result of homeowners being duped into using all of the equity in their homes to pay off their credit card debt. The problem with using equity to payoff credit card debt, is that most homeowners don't learn from their past mistakes. And they inevitably go out on another credit card buying binge that eventually forces them to default on their mortgage or deed of trust loan payments. Fact is, properties with no equity, usually end up being taken back by the lender at a public foreclosure auction or trustee's sale.

Best To Only Pursue Properties That Have A Relatively Low Debt To Value Ratio

The key to consistently making money as a pre-foreclosure property investor is to only buy properties that have a debt to value ratio of at least eighty percent. The term debt to value ratio, refers to the total amount of debt against a property in foreclosure, versus the property's current market value. For example, a property in foreclosure with $80,000 in total debt to include the principle loan balance, liens, judgments, legal fees, and loan payments, late charges and penalties in arrears, with a current market value of $105,000, would have a debt to value ratio of seventy-six percent ($80,000 in debt divided by $105,000 in current market value equals a debt to value ratio of .7619, or seventy-six percent). Personally, I never pursue a property in foreclosure, unless it has a debt to value ratio that's below seventy-five percent.

The Three Common Methods Used By Appraisers To Estimate Property Values

The three common methods used by property appraisers to estimate property values are the:
1. Comparison Sales Method: The comparison sales method, basis a property's value, on the recent sale prices of properties that are within the same area, and comparable in size, quality, amenities and features.
2. Income Method: The income method is used to estimate the value of an income producing property based on the net income the property produces.
3. Replacement Cost Method: The replacement cost method is based on what it would cost to replace the improvements on property using similar construction materials and construction methods.

Use The Comparison Sales Method To Estimate A Property's Current Value

I recommend that you use the comparison sales method to estimate a pre-foreclosure properties current market value. The comparison sales method of estimating a property's value, is based on the recent sale prices of properties within the same area, that are comparable in size, amenities and features. In order to be accurate, sale price adjustments must be made for comparable properties that have been sold at unrealistically low prices, or on overly favorable financial terms not readily available to the buying public. Comparable sales data for residential property is available online at the following Web sites:
DataQuick
www.dataquick.com
HomeGain
www.homegain.com
REAL-COMP
www.real-comp.com
HomeRadar
www.homeradar.com
Domania Home Price Check
www.domania.com

Online Sources Of Property Appraisal Information

The following Web sites have information on property appraisers and the appraisal process:

Appraisal Foundation
www.appraisalfoundation.org
Appraisal Institute
www.appraisalinstitute.org
American Society Of Appraisers
www.appraisers.org

Always Deduct The Needed Repair Costs From The Seller's Estimated Equity

As part of your due diligence, always have a thorough pre-buy property inspection done, in order to uncover all of the needed repairs. Once you have a listing of all the needed repairs, obtain repair cost estimates for each, and then deduct the total costs of all needed repairs from the seller's estimated equity. For example, if all of the needed repair cost estimates totaled $4,800, and you estimated the seller's equity to be $27,000--the property's total debt, minus its current market value--you would deduct the $4,800 in needed repair costs from the seller's $27,000 estimated equity ($27,000 equity minus $4,800 repair costs equals $22,200), which in turn would reduce the seller's estimated equity to $22,200.

Offer To Buy The Seller's Equity At A Discount Of Fifty Percent Or More

When negotiating with property owners whose loans are in default and facing imminent foreclosure, don't be afraid to make what you may personally consider to be ridiculously low, insulting offers. In many cases, you will be the seller's last resort. That is, the only person who's ready, willing and financially able to buy their property before it's sold out from underneath them, at a public foreclosure auction or trustee's sale. And they're evicted and put out onto the street, by the foreclosing lender, or the new owner. In cases where a pre-foreclosure property is vacant, I recommend that you only offer to pay the cost of reinstating the loan, paying off all recorded liens and judgments, and paying all of the closing costs. And when a property is owner-occupied, I suggest that you offer to buy the owner's equity at a discount of fifty percent or more. However, the amount you pay for an owner's equity should really depend upon the property's physical condition, and how much it's going to cost to reinstate the loan, pay-off all of the recorded liens and judgments, and repair the property to a marketable resale condition.

How I Estimate A Pre-Foreclosure Property's Current Market Value

Once I find a pre-foreclosure property with a debt to value ratio of seventy-five percent or less, I log onto the Hillsborough County Property Appraiser's Web site and type in the street address of the property in foreclosure. From the property's street address, I obtain the owner's name, mailing address, sale price and dates for the latest and prior sales, and the tax-assessed value of the property broken down by land and improvements. I also get the tax account, or folio number assigned to the property. Then I conduct an online search of the entire street that the property's located on for recent sales within the past six months. I also do an online search of adjacent streets for recent comparable sales. Next, I log onto the Hillsborough County Tax Collector's Web site, and type in the property's street address or tax folio number to obtain property tax information about the property to include any tax exemptions claimed, special tax-district assessments and the tax payment status. Once I have this information, I call my insurance broker, to get the current per square foot replacement cost, for residential properties within the same area. I recommend that you use the following four-step method that I use to estimate a pre-foreclosure property's current market value:

Step # 1: Log onto your county's property appraiser or assessor's Web site to obtain the tax assessed value of the pre-foreclosure property under consideration for purchase.

Step # 2: Search your county's property tax rolls online, for sales during the past six months of three to five similar properties, that are comparable in size, amenities and condition, and located within a one-mile radius of the property under consideration for purchase.

Step # 3: Carefully analyze comparable property sales and make price adjustments, for differences in amenities, age and physical condition, in order to estimate the property's value.

Step # 4: Calculate the per square foot cost of replacing the improvements on the property, using the same building materials and method of construction.

How To Get Free Building Replacement Cost Estimates

You can usually get a free building replacement cost estimate by calling a local independent insurance broker who represents insurers that specialize in providing property and casualty insurance coverage for residential and commercial buildings. When you call a broker, tell them that you want a replacement cost quote. Property replacement costs are calculated by using a replacement cost formula that's based on the property's geographical location and its:
1. Street address.
2. Age.
3. Type of construction.
4. Number of stories.
5. Type of roof.
6. Current use.
7. Heating and cooling system.
8. Square footage.

Online Sources For Construction Replacement Cost Calculators

The following Web sites have construction replacement cost calculators online:
Construction Cost Calculator
www.get-a-quote.net
Construction Material Calculators
www.constructionworkcenter.com/calculators.html
Building Cost Calculator
www.nt.receptive.com/rsmeans/calculator

Sample Current Market Value Worksheet

1. Tax assessed value $_____
2. Appraised value $_____
3. First mortgage or deed of trust principle loan balance $_____
4. Second mortgage or deed of trust principle loan balance $_____
5. Amount of loan payments, accrued interest, penalties and late charges in arrears $_____
6. Amount of legal fees owed $_____
7. Total amount needed to cure the default and reinstate the loan $_____
8. Amount of all liens and judgments recorded against the property $_____
9. Amount of property taxes owed $_____
10. Amount of all outstanding city, county and state fines $_____

11. Total amount owed against the property $_____
12. Property's estimated repair and cleanup costs $_____
13. Property's estimated current market value $_____
14. Cost to purchase the owner's equity at a discount of fifty percent or more $_____
15. Property search, acquisition and closing costs $_____
16. Estimated equity in property after purchase $_____

Chapter Ten

How To Negotiate With Property Owners Whose Loans Are In Default And Facing Foreclosure

How much you pay for a pre-foreclosure property pretty much depends upon how good of a negotiator you are. If you're a savvy negotiator, you can usually buy a property owner's equity, at a discount of fifty percent, or more. However, if you're a lousy negotiator, you'll probably pay way too much for your first, and most likely, last pre-foreclosure property. That's because, when you start off by overpaying for a property, you put yourself behind a "financial eight ball," that's very hard to overcome, unless you're extremely lucky and resell the property to an uninformed buyer, whose willing to pay more than it's worth. However, if you can't find an unwitting adherent to the "greater-fool-theory," your costly mistake could eventually force you to default on your mortgage or deed of trust loan and end up in foreclosure yourself.

What You Should Know About Most Property Owners In Foreclosure

First off, it has been my experience, that most of the people whose loans are in default and facing foreclosure, made a series of very bad financial decisions, that eventually led to them financial ruin. And like too many Americans today, they would rather play the blame game, than acknowledge their own financial mistakes. Secondly, most people who find themselves in this type of financial situation, usually experience some form of emotional trauma--denial, stress, fear, panic, anger and anxiety-- caused by the imminent danger of foreclosure and eviction. Plus, they often feel powerless, overwhelmed, trapped, and incapable of helping themselves solve their own financial problems. And because of their mental state of mind, most people in foreclosure can be extremely hard to deal with. That's because they usually don't act like rational, reasonable, intelligent adults. In other words, their decision-making process is based almost entirely on emotions, rather than on logic.

Most Property Owners In Foreclosure Don't Want To Sell Their Property

It may come as a surprise to many of you, but the fact is, most property owners whose loans are in default and facing foreclosure have no real interest in selling their property. Their initial interest is in trying to get the money necessary to cure the default and reinstate their loan, so they can keep their property. It's only after an owner in foreclosure finally realizes that they won't be able to "beg, borrow, or steal" the amount of money necessary to stop foreclosure, that they're willing to consider a sale.

Best To Adopt A Negotiating Style That's Compatible With Your Personality

I recommend that you adopt a negotiating style that's compatible with your personality. In other words, don't try and be what you're not. For example, if you consider yourself to be a mild-mannered, soft-spoken type of person, don't try to assume the role of a pushy, loud mouth person for the sake of negotiations. Instead, adopt a negotiating style that's compatible with your personality. This way, you can be a successful negotiator, without having to change your natural personality. I've found that most mild-mannered, soft-spoken people usually make the best negotiators, because they're generally non-confrontational and most people underestimate them at the bargaining table!

Property Owners Won't Enter Into Serious Negotiations With People They Dislike

As the old saying goes, "first impressions are lasting impressions," and this is especially true when you begin negotiating with property owners in foreclosure. The fastest way to fail, as a would-be pre-foreclosure property investor, is to come across in public as an arrogant, obnoxious, insufferable, pompous, overbearing know-it-all, with the personality of a recent honor graduate of the "Usama Bin Laden Charm School." That's because most property owners in foreclosure won't enter into serious negotiations with people whose attitude or behavior they dislike. The image that you want to project is that of a savvy polished professional investor. By "polished professional," I mean an individual who is sincere, personable, confident, knowledgeable, well spoken, well mannered, well groomed, and in control of their emotions. Lastly, never forget, that in this business, you literally get paid for being a good listener.

Don't Use Games, Gimmicks And Bullspit As Part Of Your Negotiating Strategy

Unless you aspire to join the ranks of sleazy politicians, plaintiffs' attorneys and other forms of lowlife, don't use games, gimmicks and bullspit as part of your negotiating strategy. In other words, limit the use of "tall-tales, little white lies and fibs" to describing fishing and hunting exploits, but not what you can do to help property owners in foreclosure. The fastest way to lose credibility with an owner in foreclosure is to get caught in a boldface lie. Fact is, most property owners will immediately cease negotiating with prospective buyers who try the old "dazzle them with brilliance and baffle them with bullspit" technique.

Act In An Honest, Ethical Manner When Dealing With Owners In Foreclosure

I'm a firm believer in the old adage of: "what goes around comes around!" The best advice that I can give to any pre-foreclosure property investor, is to always act in an honest, ethical manner when negotiating with property owners in foreclosure. And do as I told you to do in the introduction of this book, and always try and do what you say you're going to do, when you say you're going to do it. You must understand, that in this business, even when you do act in an honest, ethical manner, there's still a slight possibility that you could end up as a defendant in a lawsuit, accusing you of, "unjust enrichment derived from a real estate professional taking unfair advantage of a homeowner in foreclosure." In other words, a disgruntled former owner in foreclosure, files a lawsuit that claims you "screwed them," because they agreed to sell their home for less than what they thought it was worth. The best defense against these types of baseless lawsuits is to have a paper trail full of documents that prove you acted in an honest, ethical manner.

Apply The KISS Principle When Conducting Negotiations With Owners In Default

The first step in negotiating with property owners in foreclosure is to replace the myths, preconceived notions, and bad advice that they've received from well meaning, but equally ignorant friends and relatives. The best way to do this is to give the owner, a succinct, easy-to-understand explanation of the foreclosure process and how you can help them avoid it. However, please avoid using the "dazzle them with brilliance and baffle them with bullspit" technique that's commonly used by master bullspit artists, when attempting to negotiate a purchase agreement with a property owner in foreclosure. Instead, adhere to the time-tested KISS principle: keep it simple stupid, that's the basis for all military training and school lesson plans. In other words, don't go off on a long-winded, full-blown, legal-tangent when explaining how the judicial or nonjudicial foreclosure process works to an owner in foreclosure. The point here is to never forget that the object of your negotiations is to buy the owner's equity at a discount of fifty percent or more, not to impress them with your real estate expertise.

Play The Role Of Problem Solver When Negotiating With Owners In Foreclosure

I recommend that you play the role of "problem solver," when negotiating with property owners in foreclosure. By "problem solver," I mean someone whose ready, willing and able to provide immediate debt relief to owners in foreclosure. During negotiations, tell the owner that you're here to solve their problem right now! And let owners know that if they agree to sell you their property, you'll be able to close the transaction within five business days or less, depending upon their lender.

Take Control Of The Negotiating Process As Soon As You Meet With The Owner

The real key to successfully negotiating with property owners facing foreclosure is to take control of the negotiating process, as soon you meet with the owner. Here's my opening statement that I use when initially meeting face-to-face with property owners in foreclosure: *"I want to see if I can help you and help myself at the same time. Let me briefly outline how I may be able to help you solve your problem. First, I will make a financial analysis of your property. We'll go over the numbers together. If we can make a deal, there'll be no waiting. And, I'll come back to you with a written offer within twenty-four hours. But first I need to see your paperwork on the property. I need to take a look at your deed, loan documents, title insurance policy, loan payment coupon book, property tax statement and all of the letters and notices that your lender has sent you. Plus, I would like to see any property appraisal reports that you may have on hand for the property."*

As you can see from my "opening statement," I want to take control of the situation as soon as possible, in order to determine if the property is worth pursuing, and if so, what I need to do to close the sale. I suggest that you do as I do and use an owner interview worksheet like the sample copy on the following page, when conducting face-to-face interviews with property owners.

Sample Owner Interview Worksheet

Owner's name: _____
Owner's mailing address:_____
Home telephone number:_____ Work telephone number:_____
Property's street address:_____
Tax assessed value: $_____ Date of last assessment:_____
How many months are you behind on your loan payments?_____
How much do you owe in loan payments, late charges, penalties and legal fees? $_____
Type of loan: ( ) FHA ( ) VA ( ) Conventional ( ) Private
Is the loan assumable? ( ) Yes ( ) No
Monthly loan payment: Principle $_____ Interest $_____
Taxes $_____ Insurance $_____ Total payment $_____
Unpaid principle loan balance $_____
Are there any liens or judgments against the property? ( ) Yes ( ) No For how much? $_____
Do you have a recent written property appraisal? ( ) Yes ( ) No
How much did your property appraise for? $_____
Have you tried selling your property? ( ) Yes ( ) No
How long has your property been for sale?_____
Have you had any written offers yet? ( ) Yes ( ) No For how much? $_____
When is your property's scheduled foreclosure auction sale date?_____

Have The Owner Give You A "Walk-Through Tour" Of The Property

During my initial meeting with a property owner in foreclosure, I always insist on getting a "walk-through tour" of the property, prior to starting negotiations. The reason I want the owner to show me the property, is so that I can study the owner's facial expressions and tone of voice, as I ever so gently point out needed repairs. And when I notice some obvious structural defect or needed repair, I immediately bring it to the owner's attention with a comment like, "how long has this crack been in the ceiling?" Most property owners will respond with something like, "Oh my, this is the first time that I've noticed it." Sure it is! In other instances, I'll just point and shake my head or make comments to myself like, "hmm or oh boy!" I conduct "walk-through tours" to determine the interior condition of the property and to let the owner know, that I know, what's wrong with the property.

Use A No-Nonsense Approach When Negotiating With Owners In Default

My negotiating style is very direct and to the point. I know what I want, and I know what I'm willing to give to get it. And, I refuse to waste my valuable time in rambling negotiating sessions that never yield any results. To keep everything on track, I follow these five rules when conducting negotiations with owners whose mortgage or deed of trust loan is in default:

Rule #1: Never negotiate through a third party such as an attorney, accountant or real estate broker, always insist that the owner be present during all negotiations.
Rule #2: Don't act in a confrontational manner that will alienate the owner and cause negotiations to come to a screeching halt.
Rule #3: Don't assume that everything you're told by the owner is one hundred percent accurate. Take a see-it-to-believe-it attitude, and insist that all claims made about the property are supported by verifiable documentation.

Rule #4: Maintain a professional, no-nonsense demeanor that lets the owner know that you're a serious buyer who doesn't have time for games, gimmicks and bullspit!

Rule #5: Always take the path of least resistance by agreeing to mundane negotiating points that don't affect the purchase price of property, but are so important to the owner that they could kill the deal.

Eight Rules To Follow When Negotiating With Property Owners In Foreclosure

Never lose sight of the fact that buying pre-foreclosure property is a number's game. You may have to contact twenty to fifty owners whose loans are in default, before you find a pre-foreclosure property that's worth pursuing. The following eight rules were written to keep you from wasting your valuable time when negotiating with property owners whose mortgage or deed of trust loans are in default, but for whatever reason aren't ready, willing and able to sell their property yet:

Rule #1: Explain to the owner that it wouldn't be in their best interest to allow a real estate agent to tie up their property. First off, most agents wouldn't be able to close a sale before the property is foreclosed on and sold at a public foreclosure auction or trustee's auction sale. Most buyers will need to finance the purchase of the property, a process that takes too much time. Plus, lenders generally require that all needed repairs be made prior to approving any new financing. And if a property owner can't find enough money to make their monthly loan payments, they won't be able to come up with the money to make needed repairs.

Rule #2: Don't be the first person to mention a purchase price. During my experiences negotiating with property owners in foreclosure, I've found that the greatest concessions on any property's purchase price, by either buyer or seller, are usually made during the first face-to-face meeting.

Rule #3: Property owners should know as little as possible about you. It's okay to explain that you have helped other property owners avoid foreclosure, but don't tell them about your own personal financial situation or any specific properties that you've bought. However, always mention that you have other properties under consideration for purchase. It's important to let owners know that your time and funds are limited, and that they need to make a decision promptly. Never give any property owner more than twenty-four hours in which to make a decision about selling the equity in their property. However, let property owners know that further negotiations can be resumed at a later date, but the offer just discussed wouldn't apply then.

Rule #4: When walking through the property with the owner, gently point out any needed repairs. The owner must know that you know that the property is far from perfect and that all of the problems you point out will be reflected in the price being discussed.

Rule #5: In some cases, a property owner may say he has a better offer pending. When you hear such a claim being made, it's always best to say: "Then why didn't you accept the offer?" However, remind the owner that because of their circumstances, time is of the essence. And if they have a better deal pending, than what you intend to offer, they should take it! Always call their bluff. They either have a real offer, at which time they'll take it if it's better than your offer, or they don't.

Rule #6: Never leave an unsigned purchase agreement with an owner. If you do, you're inviting them to use your offer, as a negotiating tool with the next buyer. If you fail to get a signed purchase agreement on your initial visit, add the owner's name to your "tickler file" and make a note to contact them in ten days.

Rule #7: Have a set agenda. Don't let negotiations go on forever. Once the deal is final, it's final! Make sure that the owner fully understands there's no: "can-we-do-this-later-on?" Because after the purchase agreement is signed, it's a legal and binding contract and you aren't going to re-negotiate anything.

Rule #8: Don't negotiate with people who can't make the final decision. Find out right up front, before negotiations begin, if the party that you're dealing with is in a position to make a final decision once you start negotiations. This is especially true when dealing with married couples or "partners." If someone you begin negotiations with claims to have a spouse or a partner, tell them that the only way you'll continue negotiations is if you can sit down, face-to-face, with the both of them

Offer Debt Relief To Owners With Vacant Properties In Foreclosure

In many cases, owners in foreclosure have moved out and abandoned their property. They assume, incorrectly, that by moving away from the property, they can leave their financial obligations behind. In cases where a pre-foreclosure property is vacant, offer the owner debt relief and the opportunity to keep a foreclosure from appearing on their consumer credit files. An offer of debt relief means that you agree to pay the lender, the amount of money that's needed, to cure the default and reinstate the loan.

Offer Debt Relief And A "Moving Allowance" For Owner-Occupied Properties

When you locate a pre-foreclosure property that's owner-occupied, but with a loan that'll cost more than $5,000 to reinstate and other liens and judgments recorded against its title, I suggest that you offer the owner debt relief, along with a $1,500 to $2,500 cash "moving allowance."

Offer To Buy The Owner's Equity For Fifty Cents Or Less On The Dollar

Lastly, on the very few occasions when you do find a pre-foreclosure property that's in good physical condition, with a loan that'll cost less than $5,000 to reinstate, and no other liens or judgments recorded against its title, I recommend that you offer to buy the owner's equity for fifty cents or less on the dollar.

Chapter Eleven

How To Get Subordinate Lienholders To Discount Their Liens By Fifty Percent Or More

In chapter five, I gave you the lowdown on how to perform due diligence to uncover all liens and judgments attached to a pre-foreclosure property's title. Now, I'm going to tell you how to negotiate with subordinate or "junior" lienholders. As far as I'm concerned, the real "hallmark" of a profitable pre-foreclosure property investor, is the ability to get subordinate lienholders to discount their liens by fifty percent or more. That's because in this business, your profit margin is tied directly to how well you're able to negotiate discounts with subordinate leinholders. However, in order to obtain substantial discounts from subordinate lienholders, you must first know how to:
1. Identify subordinate lienholders of record.
2. Verify a subordinate lien's validity.
4. Contact subordinate lienholders of record.
5. Negotiate lien discounts of fifty percent or more.
5. Contest fraudulent liens in a court of competent jurisdiction.
6. Have liens removed from a property's title.

The Difference Between A Judgment Lien And A Lien

The difference between a judgment lien that's placed against a judgment debtor's property for failure to repay a debt and a lien such as a mortgage or deed of trust is as follows:
1. Judgment lien. A judgment lien is a formal written decree, issued by a court of competent jurisdiction that declares a judgment debtor to be indebted to a judgment creditor.
2. Lien. A lien is a legal claim that a creditor places against the title to real and personal property of a debtor, as security for the repayment of a debt.

Five Most Common Types Of Subordinate Liens That Attach To Real Property

The five most common types of subordinate liens that attach to the titles of real property are:
1. Second and third Mortgage or deed of trust liens.
2. Judgment liens.
3. Mechanic's liens.
5. State and federal welfare, medical and child support liens.
4. Local, state and federal tax liens.

States Require That Subordinate Lienholders Be Notified Of Foreclosure Action

As far as I know, all state foreclosure statutes require, that all subordinate or junior lienholders of record, be notified when a senior lienholder files a foreclosure lawsuit or notice of default to foreclose on a mortgage or deed of trust loan. The subordinate lienholder notification requirement is supposed to protect subordinate lienholders from having their liens extinguished by foreclosure, without first having the opportunity to defend their lien.

Subordinate Lienholders Are Named As Defendants In Foreclosure Lawsuits

When a lender files a foreclosure lawsuit, all subordinate lienholders of record are named as defendants in the complaint, and notice of lis pendens and served with a copy of the foreclosure lawsuit. You can obtain the names and addresses of subordinate lienholders of record that are named as defendants in a foreclosure lawsuit, simply by going to the clerk of your county or circuit court, and requesting the foreclosure case file. Most clerks' offices have public reading rooms where people can sit and read documents that have been filed with the court.

Trustees Required To Send Subordinate Lienholders Copies Of Notice Of Default

Most state foreclosure statutes require trustees foreclosing on deeds of trust, to send a copy of the notice of default to each subordinate lienholder of record. That's because, the names of subordinate lienholders aren't listed on notices of default. The three parties that are listed on a notice of default are the borrower-trustor, beneficiary-lender and the trustee that's foreclosing on the deed of trust.

Subordinate Lienholders Aren't Always Notified Of Foreclosure Actions

First off, never automatically assume that all subordinate lienholders of record have been notified about a foreclosure action by the senior lienholder foreclosing on a mortgage or deed of trust loan. Because if you do, and a senior lienholder fails to uncover all subordinate liens of record, prior to filing a foreclosure lawsuit or notice of default, you could be in for a very expensive surprise, after you've bought the property. To illustrate my point, let's suppose that you ignored my advice in chapter five, and failed to perform your own due diligence, and bought a pre-foreclosure property, without having a title search done. And because you assumed that all of the subordinate liens, recorded against the property's title, had been uncovered by the foreclosing lender, you went ahead and bought the property, for what you thought at the time was a bargain-basement price. However, when you were in the process of reselling the property, you received the surprise of your life, when a search of the property's title revealed a $15,000 mechanic's lien that the foreclosing lender had somehow overlooked. Now, what you had thought was the "bargain of a lifetime," has turned into a breakeven deal, at best. All of this could've easily been avoided by spending $125 to $175 for a title search by a competent title abstractor.

Become Familiar With Your State's Lien Law

I very highly recommend that you take the time and effort to become familiar with your state's lien law. In particular, you must know how:
1. Long judgment liens stay attached to real property titles.
2. Long judgment liens can be renewed for.
3. Which parties are authorized to a file a mechanic's lien.
4. Long a mechanic's lien stays attached to real property titles.
5. Long a mechanic's lien can be renewed for.

Unlicensed Contractors Have No Lien Rights In Most States

Most state construction lien laws prohibit unlicensed contractors and repairmen from filing any type of lien. For example, if an unlicensed contractor or repairmen worked on a property and for whatever reason they didn't get paid, they couldn't legally record a mechanic's lien against the property's title. However, if they did file a lien, they wouldn't be able to enforce it in court.

Most Local, State And Federal Government Agencies Won't Discount Their Liens

It has been my experience, that most local, state and federal government agencies won't discount their liens. However, under certain circumstances, I've been able to negotiate discounts on federal tax liens and city and county code enforcement liens.

How To Apply To Have A Federal Tax Lien Removed From A Property's Title

Internal Revenue Service publication number 783, is available at the Web page listed below, and has instructions on how to apply for a certificate of discharge of property from a federal tax lien.
Internal Revenue Service Publication 783
http://www.irs.gov/pub/irs-pdf/p783.pdf

Internal Revenue Service Office Location Nationwide

For a listing of Internal Revenue Service office locations nationwide, log onto the Web page listed below:
Internal Revenue Service Offices
http://www.irs.gov/localcontacts/#stateLinks

Verify All Judgment Or "Name Liens" To Determine Their Validity

A judgment lien that's recorded and indexed in the public records, under the name of a judgment debtor and not under the legal description of real property is often referred to as a "name lien." The reason why you must verify all judgment liens is because the name of a judgment debtor that's listed in a lien document may be the exact same name as a borrower in foreclosure, but it belongs to a different person altogether.

How To Verify That A Judgment Lien Is Valid

First off, if the judgment lien document has the judgment debtor's social security account number, or driver license number listed on it, you can use them to verify the judgment debtor's full legal name. Or, if there's a legal description listed in a judgment lien, you can compare it to the legal description that's listed on the deed of the property in foreclosure. Lastly, if a judgment lien document lists only a street address where the judgment creditor believed that the judgment debtor named in the lien lived at the time the lien was recorded, you can compare the street address to the street address of the property in foreclosure.

In Most States Recording A Fraudulent Lien Constitutes "Slander of Title"

In most states, recording a fraudulent lien against the title to real property is considered, "slander of title" and a civil offense. As an example, let's suppose that another investor, whose a competitor of yours, records a bogus option agreement against the title of a property that you have under contract for the sole purpose of "creating a cloud on the property's title." In most states, this would be considered "slander of title" and grounds for a civil lawsuit.

How To Contest The Validity Of A Judgment Lien

I recommend that you contest any judgment lien that you suspect is fraudulent. For example, in Florida, a lien's validity can be contested by filing a notice of contest of lien like the sample copy below in a court of competent jurisdiction. Once a notice is filed, a lienholder has sixty days from the date the notice is served to file a lawsuit to enforce their lien. And if a lienholder fails to respond to the notice of contest of lien within the sixty-day period, or fails to prove the lien's validity in court, the judge presiding over the case, will issue an order removing the lien from the property's title.

Sample Florida Notice Of Contest Of Lien

STATE OF FLORIDA
COUNTY OF HILLSBOROUGH

To: John I. Crook
    69 Sleazy Way
    Tampa, FL 33689

You are notified that the undersigned contests the claim of lien filed by you on January 3, 2000 and recorded in Official Records Book 4567, Page 123, of the public records of Hillsborough County, Florida, and that the time within which you may file suit to enforce your lien is limited to 60 days from the date of service of this notice.

DATED on this tenth day of August 2003.

                                                David D. Jones
                                                Plaintiff

Compile Information About Each Subordinate Lienholder

I recommend that you use a subordinate lienholder worksheet, like the copy below, to compile information on each subordinate lienholder:

Sample Subordinate Lienholder Worksheet

Lienholder's name:_____
Mailing address:_____
Telephone number:_____
Facsimile number:_____
E-mail address:_____
Type of lien:_____
Amount of lien:_____
Date lien recorded:_____
Date lienholder contacted:_____
Comments:_____

Best To Contact Subordinate Lienholders By Letter

Once you've identified, of all of the subordinate lienholders of record, send each one a letter, like the sample copy below, offering to buy their lien at a discounted price, of fifty percent or more.

Sample Letter To Subordinate Lienholders

Mr. Ralph R. Rowdy
6178 Bowler Avenue
Brandon, FL 33508

Dear Mr. Rowdy:

I'm writing to you in regards to your $1,346.89 judgment lien, that's recorded against the title to Mr. Robert F. Default's property, located at 3345 Costa Rosa Way, Tampa, FL 33649.

You should've already been notified, that The Bank of Florida, has filed a foreclosure lawsuit against Mr. Robert F. Default, in Hillsborough County Circuit Court, to foreclose their mortgage loan, that's secured by the property located at 3345 Costa Rosa Way, Tampa, FL 33649.

The public foreclosure auction sale is scheduled for September 10, 2003, at 11 A.M., on the second floor lobby of the Hillsborough County Courthouse.

I'm sure you already know that if Mr. Default is unable to bring his mortgage payments current and the Bank of Florida does forecloses on his loan, your judgment lien will be extinguished and you'll receive nothing in the process.

I'm currently in negotiations with Mr. Default, to possibly purchase his property, before the Bank of Florida forecloses on their mortgage loan and all subordinate liens are wiped out.

However, the only way that I'll be able to purchase Mr. Debtor's property, and stop the Bank of Florida from foreclosing on their loan, is if judgment lienholders are willing to sell their liens to me at a sixty percent discount.

Please let me know at your earliest convenience, if you accept my offer to purchase your judgment lien for $538.76.

You may call me at (813) 123-4567, or e-mail me at davidjones@hotmail.com.

Sincerely,

David D. Jones

Most Subordinate Lienholders Will Sell Their Liens At A Discounted Price

I've found that most--more than eighty percent---of all subordinate lienholders, are willing to sell their liens at a discounted price. They know that half of nothing is nothing, but that half of a dollar is fifty cents. Fact is most subordinate lienholders are thrilled to get fifty cents on the dollar for their liens. Plus, very few lienholders have the time, money or desire to fight senior lienholders in court.

What To Say During Face-To-Face Negotiations With Subordinate Lienholders

The main point that you must always stress during face-to-face negotiations with subordinate lienholders, is that if the property is sold at a public foreclosure auction or trustee's sale, their lien will be wiped out and they'll end up with absolutely nothing. During your discussions with lienholders, you must explain to them why it's in their best financial interest to sell you their lien today at a discounted price, rather than have their lien extinguished by a foreclosure action. As far as I'm concerned, your goal during negotiations should always be to push a lienholder's "panic and greed buttons," so that they get up off of their duff and sell you their lien at a discount of fifty percent or more. In other words, use their fear of losing everything to "scare" them into selling you their lien!

What To Do When A Subordinate Lienholder Refuses Your Initial Offer

You have five options when a subordinate lienholder refuses your initial offer to buy their lien at a discount. You can:
1. Make a counteroffer to buy the lien for ten percent more than your initial offer.
2. Keep making counteroffers until one is accepted.
3. Give in and pay the full amount of the lien.
4. Buy the property with the lien still attached to its title.
5. Throw in the towel and not buy the property.

Have All Subordinate Lienholders Sign A Satisfaction Of Lien That's Recordable

Lastly, whatever you do don't payoff any subordinate lienholders until after the title to the property has been transferred into your name and recorded in the public records. And when you do payoff a subordinate lienholder, have them sign a satisfaction of lien that's in a recordable form, in the presence of a notary public. Once that's done, record the satisfaction of lien in the public records of the county where the property's deed is recorded.

Chapter Twelve

Everything You Need To Know About Short Payoff Sales: What They Are, How They Work And When To Use Them

I've included this chapter on the much-ballyhooed short payoff sale acquisition technique, to try and counteract the myths, lies and fairytales that are currently being spread around by self-professed short sale gurus! Over the past year and a half, it seems like everyone and his brother has jumped onto the short payoff sale bandwagon. To hear the short sale promoters tell it, you'd think that short sales were the greatest real estate acquisition techniques, since the "nothing down" graze of the early 1980s! The problem with ninety-nine percent of the short sales hype that's currently being foisted onto an unsuspecting public, by unscrupulous real estate hucksters peddling overpriced courses and boot camp seminars, is that it's based on misinformation, half-truths, distortions and outright lies. All of this hype has fueled unrealistic expectations on the part of would-be short sale investors, who've been led to believe, that every lender in America will approve a short payoff sale, at the drop of a hat. I hate to be a party pooper, but that's unadulterated bullspit! And that's why in this chapter, I'm going to tell you the unvarnished truth about short payoff sales. I'm also going to give you complete step-by-step instructions on exactly how the short payoff of a mortgage or deed of trust loan actually works.

The Definition Of A "Short Payoff Sale"

A "short payoff sale," is generally defined by loan loss mitigation professionals, as: *"A sale in which a lender allows the property securing a mortgage or deed of trust loan to be sold for less than the existing loan balance, due to factors such as the borrower's financial circumstances, the property's physical condition and local real estate market conditions."*

Short Payoff Sales Are Lenders Last Resort Before Proceeding With Foreclosure

First things first: In spite of what the self-professed "short sale pros and experts" may espouse, bona fide short payoff sale transactions, are very few and far between. In fact, most lenders will only approve a short payoff sale as a last resort, when foreclosure isn't economically feasible because the borrower is insolvent, and:
1. The property was purchased or refinanced at the top of a seller's market at an over-inflated price, and has had a substantial drop in value.
2. The property was refinanced at one hundred and twenty-five percent of its value that was based on an over-inflated property appraisal report.
3. The property is located in an area where property values have dropped due to a dramatic change in local economic conditions.
4. The property's value has decreased to an amount that's below the loan balance due to local and national economic conditions, that are beyond the borrower's control.
5. The property's "as is" condition has deteriorated to the point where it's not financially feasible for the lender, to put it in a marketable resale condition.
6. The proposed purchase price is more than the lender would be able to sell the property for after foreclosing on the loan.
7. Any sales commission the lender must pay is less than what they would have pay to sell the property after foreclosing on the loan.

Most Lenders Have A Stringent "Hardship Test" That Borrowers Must Pass

Contrary to what the short sale seminar promoters would lead you to believe, most lenders have a stringent "hardship test" that borrowers must pass in order to have the short payoff of their loan approved. In most cases, the borrower must be experiencing one or more of the following financial hardships:
1. The borrower, or an immediate member of the borrower's family has experienced a catastrophic illness that has wreaked havoc on their personal finances.
2. The borrower's spouse has died or divorced and they have insufficient income to pay the loan payment.
3. The borrower 's employer has transferred them out of the area and they're unable to sell or rent the property.
4. The borrower has been called away to active duty military service for an extended period and lacks the monthly income to pay their loan.
5. The borrower has suffered a disabling injury that precludes them from ever working again.
6. The borrower is unemployed and has no realistic expectations of finding employment in the foreseeable future, due to local economic conditions that are beyond their control.
7. The borrower has become financially insolvent, and there's no realistic expectation that their financial condition will improve within the foreseeable future.
8. The borrower has been incarcerated and no longer has the income to pay the loan payment.

Factors That Influence A Lender's Willingness To Approve Short Payoff Sales

The following factors, generally influence a lender's willingness to approve a short payoff sale:
1. The number of nonperforming loans that the lender has in their portfolio.
2. The lender's overall financial condition.
3. The financial condition of the third party investor who owns the loan.

4. The loss mitigation policy of the third party investor who owns the loan.
5. The loss mitigation authority of the lender servicing the loan.
6. The loss mitigation policy and procedures of the government agency insuring or guaranteeing the loan.

Six Factors Lenders Consider During The Short Payoff Sale Approval Process

When deciding whether or not to approve a short payoff sale, lenders consider the following six factors:
Factor #1: The borrower's overall financial condition.
Factor #2: The property's "as is" value.
Factor #3: The cost to put the property into resale condition.
Factor #4: The property's "as repaired" value.
Factor #5: The cost of securing and maintaining the property while it's being marketed for resale.
Factor #6: The cost of marketing and selling the property.

How Private Mortgage Insurance Can Effect A Short Payoff Sale

Private mortgage insurance (PMI) is purchased by institutional lenders--and paid for by borrowers--to insure against a lender's loss in the event that a loan is foreclosed on. The reason why institutional lenders require borrowers to pay premiums for private mortgage insurance coverage, is because conventional residential loans have a high loan to value ratio (LTV), which doesn't give lenders enough of an equity cushion to compensate them when a loan is foreclosed on. This way, if the lender recoups less than the balance owed from the proceeds of a public foreclosure auction or trustee's sale, the private mortgage insurance company must pay a claim up to the amount of the coverage. Once a lender declares a loan that's covered by private mortgage insurance to be in default, the insurer could:
1. Advance the borrower the funds needed to cure the default and reinstate the loan.
2. Purchase the loan from the lender and modify the repayment terms to match the borrower's current income.
3. Approve the short sale and reimburse the lender for their loss, up to the amount of the coverage.

Final Short Sale Approval Must Come From The Investor Owning The Loan

In almost all most cases, the lender or loss mitigation company that's servicing a loan in default isn't authorized to approve a short payoff sale. That's because final approval for a short payoff sale usually must come from the investor who actually owns the loan. And oftentimes, it can take thirty days, or longer for an investor like Fannie Mae or Freddie Mac to approve a short payoff sale.

Most Lenders Turn Loans In Default Over To Loan Loss Mitigation Specialists

Once a lender declares a loan to be in default, it's usually turned over to a special department, or a separate company that specializes in loan loss mitigation. Fact is, there's a whole industry that specializes in loan loss mitigation, loan foreclosure and lenders' other real estate owned or OREO. They handle everything from filing foreclosure lawsuits and notices of default to protecting properties in foreclosure from vandalism. The following is a listing of the various names that are given to the department that handles loans that are in default:
1. Loan loss mitigation department.

2. Default management department.
3. Loan workout department.
4. Loan resolution department.
5. Nonperforming assets department.
6. Foreclosure department.
7. Collections department.
8. Special loans department.

Federal Housing Administration Short Sales Are Called Pre-Foreclosure Sales

Short payoff sales are known in the Department of Housing and Urban Renewal (HUD), as "pre-foreclosure sales." Pre-foreclosure sales of Federal Housing Administration (FHA) insured loans are covered in HUD Mortgagee Letter 00-05, dated January 19, 2000. The only lenders authorized to approve a short payoff or pre-foreclosure sale, of an FHA insured loan, are "loss mitigation lenders" that have been approved by HUD. In order to be eligible for a pre-foreclosure sale, the:
1. Property securing the loan in default must be owner-occupied.
2. Loan must be at least ninety days in arrears.
3. Borrower must have a bona fide financial hardship.
4. Borrower must receive counseling from a HUD approved agency.

Federal Housing Administration Short Payoff Sale Information Available Online

Federal Housing Administration (FHA), pre-foreclosure sale information is available online, at the Web site, listed below:
FHA Pre-Foreclosure Sale Information
www.hudclips.org/sub_nonhud/html/pdfforms/00-05.doc

Toll-Free Telephone Number For The FHA National Loan Servicing Center

The toll-free telephone number for the FHA National Loan Servicing center, is listed below:
FHA National Loan Servicing Center
(888) 297-8685

Department Of Veterans Affairs Short Payoff Sales Are Called Compromise Sales

The Department of Veterans Affairs (DVA) calls short payoff sales "compromise sales." A compromise sale, of a DVA guaranteed loan is approved when the DVA considers a loan default to be "insoluble." The DVA will consider a default insoluble when a review of the borrower's financial circumstances indicates that the borrower lacks the ability to prevent foreclosure of the loan and at the same time provide for the welfare of their family.

Department Of Veterans Affairs Compromise Sale Information Available Online

Department of Veterans Affairs (DVA), compromise sale information is available online at the Web site, listed below:
DVA Compromise Sale Information
www.vba-roanoke.com/rlc/forms/Compromise%20Sale%20Program.pdf

Department Of Veterans Affairs (DVA) Regional Loan Centers

The following is a listing of Department of Veterans Affairs (DVA) regional loan centers and the states they serve:

Atlanta, GA
(888) 768-2132
Georgia, North Carolina, South Carolina, Tennessee

Cleveland, OH
(800) 729-5772
Delaware, Indiana, Michigan, New Jersey, Ohio, Pennsylvania

Denver, CO
(888) 349-7541
Alaska, Colorado, Idaho, Montana, New Mexico, Oregon, Utah, Washington, Wyoming

Houston, TX
(888) 232-2571
Arkansas, Louisiana, Oklahoma, Texas

Manchester, NH
(603) 666-7502
Connecticut, Maine, Massachusetts, New Hampshire, New York, Rhode Island, Vermont

Phoenix, AZ
(888) 869-0194
Arizona, California, Nevada

Roanoke, VA
(800) 933-5499
District of Columbia, Kentucky, Maryland, Virginia, West Virginia

St. Paul, MN
(800) 827-0611
Illinois, Iowa, Kansas, Minnesota, Missouri, Nebraska, North Dakota, South Dakota, Wisconsin

St. Petersburg, FL
(888) 611-5916 x7500
Alabama, Florida, Mississippi

Hawaii
(808) 433-0480

Puerto Rico
(787) 772-7313

The Fifteen Steps Necessary To Complete A Short Payoff Sale Transaction

A short payoff sale transaction typically takes the following fifteen steps to complete:

Step #1: The buyer contacts a property owner in foreclosure and determines that the borrower's financial situation and the property's physical condition make it a potential short payoff sale candidate.

Step #2: The borrower gives the investor written authorization to contact the loan loss mitigation department, currently servicing the loan.

Step #3: The buyer contacts the loan loss mitigation department that's listed on the latest correspondence that the borrower has received from the lender to obtain the name, e-mail address and telephone and facsimile numbers of the person in charge.

Step #4: The buyer sends the person in charge of the loan loss mitigation department a facsimile of the borrower's authorization to release loan information letter.

Step #5: The buyer calls the person in charge of the loan loss mitigation department to discuss the current status of the borrower's loan and to request a short payoff sale package, for the borrower.
Step #6: The borrower receives the short payoff sale package along with the lender's instruction on how to complete it.
Step #7: The borrower obtains all of the documentation that the lender requires to support their financial hardship.
Step #8: The buyer obtains the repair cost estimates from three licensed home improvement contractors.
Step #9: The buyer obtains the addresses and sale prices of similar properties, that are located in the same area, that have sold within the past six months along with the addresses and asking prices of properties that are currently for sale.
Step #10: The buyer returns the short payoff sale package to the lender via courier. The package includes a signed purchase agreement to buy the property, for forty percent less that what's owed the lender.
Step #11: The lender reviews the short payoff sale package and orders a broker's price opinion or property appraisal report to determine the property's "as is and "as repaired" values.
Step #12: The lender makes a decision to accept or refuse the short payoff based on the property's value and physical condition.
Step #13: The lender refuses the buyer's initial short payoff offer based on the BPO or property appraisal.
Step #14: The buyer makes the lender a counteroffer that's either accepted or refused.
Step #15: The buyer closes on the short payoff transaction thirty days after the offer was accepted.

The Four Parties That Are Usually Involved In A Short Sale Transaction

The four parties that are usually involved in a short payoff sale transaction, are the:
1. Property owner whose loan is in default and facing foreclosure.
2. Party buying the property that's securing the loan in default.
3. Investor who owns the loan in default.
4. Third party servicing the loan in default.

Two Main Reasons Why Property Owners Won't Agree To A Short Payoff Sale

The two main reasons, why most property owners in foreclosure, won't agree to a short payoff sale, are that:
1. Lenders don't allow property owners, to receive any of the proceeds, from a short payoff sale.
2. The amount of debt, that's cancelled, by the short payoff of a mortgage or deed of trust loan is subject to federal income tax, as ordinary earned income. However, cancelled debt is not taxable, when the borrower is bankrupt or deemed insolvent, by the IRS.

Investors Need Cash Or Credit To Finance Short Payoff Sale Transactions

One key point about short payoff sales that's often overlooked is that investors need cash or credit to finance the transaction. That's because ninety-nine percent of all lenders will not sign a purchase agreement that contains an assignment clause. Plus, most lenders require a verifiable "proof of funds letter," stating the source of the funds needed to buy the property.

All Lenders Require That Short Payoff Sales Be "Arms Length" Transactions

Virtually all lenders require that all short payoff sales be what's called, an "arm's length transaction." The term, "arms length transaction," means that a relative or close friend of a property owner in default, can't be a party to a short payoff sale transaction.

I Require That The Loan Balance Be Discounted By At Least Thirty Percent

As far as I'm concerned, short payoff sales are too time consuming and generally a royal pain in the keister! Plus, you're forced to deal with the ignoramuses that makeup the staffs of most loan loss mitigation departments. And if I'm going to have my money tied up in a property, I want to get a good return on my investment. That's why I won't complete a short sale transaction, unless the lender is willing to discount the loan balance by at least thirty percent.

Persistence Is The Crucial Ingredient Needed To Complete A Short Payoff Sale

Trust me, you don't need to buy a thirty-page, "short sale primer" for $189, or attend an overpriced "short sale boot camp," in order to successfully complete, a short payoff sale transaction. However, what you do need in addition to specialized knowledge, and money or access to money, is perseverance, and a very heavy dose of patience! And oftentimes during a short payoff sale transaction, it can seem like the stars must be in perfect alignment with the moon, in order for the sale to close! I've found that most people fail to complete a short payoff sale, because they get discouraged and usually quit, when they can't get passed the bimbo or bozo answering the telephone, in the loan loss mitigation department. Don't be a quitter!

How To Quickly Determine The Feasibility Of Attempting A Short Payoff Sale

It has been my experience that less than five percent of all properties in foreclosure, qualify for a short payoff sale. That's why, before you invest the time and effort that's necessary to put a credible short payoff sale package together, you must first know the:
1. Total amount of all liens recorded against the property's title.
2. Lender's loan loss mitigation policy.
3. Borrower's current financial condition.
4. Type of loan in default.
5. Current status of the loan in default.
6. Property's "as is" market value.
7. Property's "as repaired" value.
8. Local economic and real estate market conditions.

Obtain The Borrower's Written Authorization To Release Loan Information

Once you've determined that an owner's financial situation and a property's physical condition have a better than average chance of meeting a lender's short payoff sale approval criteria, you must have the borrower sign a letter of authorization to release loan information, like the sample copy on the following page. This will authorize the lender to discuss the borrower's loan, with the third party named in the letter.

Sample Borrower's Letter Of Authorization To Release Loan Information

I, Robert D. Default, hereby authorize the Bank of Florida, to discuss and release all of the financial information concerning my mortgage loan, loan number: FL08281950 on my property located at 3345 Costa Rosa Way, Tampa, Florida 33649, to David D. Jones.
Sincerely,

Robert D. Default
Mortgagor
3345 Costa Rosa Way
Tampa, FL 33649

Most Lenders Use A Broker's Price Opinion To Determine A Property's Value

The term "broker's price opinion" or BPO refers to the appraisal format that real estate licensees use to appraise property for lenders. Most major lenders have their own broker's price opinion forms that they require licensees to use. However, most lenders won't order a broker's price opinion or property appraisal report, until after they've received a complete short payoff sale package to include all of the documentation that's required to support the borrower's financial condition. I've included a copy of the Fannie Mae Broker's Price Opinion form at the end of this chapter, so that you can see the appraisal criteria that lenders use to value property. Lenders order broker's price opinions or appraisal reports to determine a property's:
1. "As is" value.
2. "As repaired" value.

Include A "Short Payoff Sale Proposal Letter" In The Short Sale Package

I highly recommend that you always include, a short payoff sale proposal letter, like the sample copy below, in the borrower's short payoff sale package, that's submitted to lenders.

Sample Short Payoff Sale Proposal Letter

Ms. Sally S. Short
Manager
Loan Loss Mitigation Department
Bank of Florida
4467 Rich Avenue
Clearwater, FL 33227

Reference Loan Number: FL08281950, Robert D. Default, Mortgagor, 3345 Costa Rosa Way, Tampa, Florida 33649

Dear Ms. Short:

Please find enclosed the short payoff sale package for loan number: FL08281950, Robert D. Default, mortgagor, 3345 Costa Rosa Way, Tampa, Florida 33649

My proposed purchase price of $ 90,000, is based upon the following facts:

1. Based on the recent sale of comparable properties within the same area the "as is" sale price for the property is between $88,000 and $92,000 (see the attached listing of comparable property addresses).
2. Based on repair cost estimates, from three-licensed home repair contractors, it will cost between $18,000 and $25,000 to repair the property to a marketable resale condition (see the attached repair cost estimates).
3. The borrower is insolvent.
4. Property values within the area surrounding the subject property have declined by over twenty percent, in the past two years.
Lastly, I have the funds on hand to close on the purchase of the property within twenty-four hours notice.
Please call me at (813) 123-4567, or e-mail me at davidjones@hotmail.com if you have any questions.

Sincerely,

David D. Jones

Prepare A Preliminary "Net Sheet" On A HUD 1 Settlement Statement Form

Most lenders generally require buyers to submit a net sheet as part of their short payoff sale package. Lenders use net sheets to calculate how much money they'll net from the proceeds of a proposed short sale. A word of caution: When calculating a net sheet, make certain that the seller's net proceeds from the sale are zero. I recommend that you prepare the lender's "net sheet," on a HUD 1 Settlement Statement form, like the sample copy at the end of this chapter.

HUD 1 Settlement Statement Available Online

You can fill out a HUD 1 Settlement Statement online at the Web page listed below:
HUD 1 Settlement Statement
http://www.hudclips.org/sub_nonhud/html/pdfforms/1.pdf

A Loan Sold Short Is Cancelled Debt That's Subject To Federal Income Tax

Under the Internal Revenue Code, a mortgage or deed of trust loan that's sold short, or discounted by $600 or more, is considered to be a cancelled debt that's subject to federal income tax as ordinary earned income. And when a lender accepts a short payoff on a mortgage or deed of trust loan that's for $600 or more, the lender must report the sale to the Internal Revenue Service on Internal Revenue Service Form 1099C, Cancellation of Debt. Internal Revenue Service Publication number 544, *Sales and Other Dispositions Of Assets,* that's available at the Web page listed below, explains in detail how cancelled debt is taxed.
Sales and Other Dispositions Of Assets
http://www.irs.gov/pub/irs-pdf/p544.pdf

How The Internal Revenue Service Defines "Insolvency"

The Internal Revenue Service defines "insolvency" as follows: *"You are insolvent when, and to the extent, your liabilities exceed the fair market value of your assets."*

I Tell The Property Owner About The Tax Consequences Of A Short Payoff Sale

I'm a firm believer in always acting in an honest, ethical manner during any type of business transaction. In fact, I always try and go "above and beyond the call of duty," when I'm involved in a real estate transaction with owners in foreclosure. When discussing a potential short payoff sale, I always tell the property owner upfront that the amount of debt that the lender cancels will be taxed as ordinary income, unless the borrower is bankrupt or insolvent. I also give the owner copies of Internal Revenue Service Publication number 544, *Sales and Other Dispositions Of Assets*, and number 908, *Bankruptcy Tax Guide*.

Best To Use A Checklist When Preparing A Short Payoff Sale Package

I recommend that you use a checklist when assisting a property owner, in the preparation of a short payoff sale package. Your checklist should include the following items:
1. Buyer's letter of short payoff sale proposal.
2. Borrower's signed letter of authorization for the lender to release financial information about the loan in default to the buyer.
3. Borrower's completed and signed short payoff sale application.
4. Borrower's hardship letter.
5. Borrower's financial statement.
6. Borrower's payroll check-stubs from employer.
7. Borrower's financial history.
8. Borrower's unemployment compensation insurance coverage payment history.
9. Borrower's state and federal income tax returns for the past two-years.
10. Borrower's bank statements for the past six months.
11. Copies of the borrower's consumer credit files from Equifax, Experian and Trans Union credit reporting agencies.
12. Summary of any medical illnesses, to include treatment costs for any illnesses that the borrower may be currently suffering from.
13. Copies of any divorce decree showing borrower's financial obligations for child support or alimony payments.
14. Completed and signed purchase agreement.
15. A listing of comparable sales of similar properties within the same area.
17. HUD 1 Settlement Statement.
18. Itemized listing of repairs and the cost of putting the property into a marketable resale condition.
19. Pictures of the property's "as is" condition.

Most Real Estate Licensees Don't Know Diddly-Squat About Short Payoff Sales

Lastly, most properties in foreclosure aren't listed for sale with real estate brokers. That's because, most real estate brokers refuse to list properties that are in foreclosure. They do this, because they fear that the property will be sold at a public foreclosure auction, or trustee's sale before they can find a buyer, and they'll end up with nothing to show for their time and effort. Secondly, based on my experiences with real estate licensees, what most of them know about the foreclosure process and short payoff sales, would fit into a thimble! Fact is, most real estate licensees, don't know diddly squat, about, short payoff sales. And that's exactly why, I recommend that you never attempt a short payoff sale on any property that's listed for sale with a real estate broker.

Case No. _____
File No. _____

BROKER'S PRICE OPINION

FannieMae

PROPERTY ADDRESS: _____
City _____ County _____ State ____ Zip _____
REO# _____ FIRM NAME _____

FANNIE MAE SALES REP _____ COMPLETED BY _____

DATE _____ PHONE NO. _____

This BPO will have a significant impact on the marketing of this property. Every effort should be made to provide accurate and detailed information in your evaluation. Comments are always welcome and are usually necessary to describe the property and market.

I. GENERAL MARKET CONDITIONS

Current market conditions: ☐ Depressed ☐ Slow ☐ Stable ☐ Improving ☐ Excellent
Employment conditions: ☐ Declining ☐ Stable ☐ Increasing
Market price of this type property has:
  ☐ Decreased _____ % in past _____ months.
  ☐ Increased _____ % in past _____ months.
  ☐ Remained Stable

Estimated percentage of owners vs tenants in neighborhood: _____ % owner occupant _____ % tenant
There is a: ☐ normal supply ☐ oversupply ☐ shortage of comparable listings in the neighborhood.
Approximate number of comparable units for sale in neighborhood: _____
No. of competing listings in neighborhood that are REO or Corporate owned: _____
No. of boarded or blocked-up homes: _____
COMMENTS: _____
_____
_____

II. SUBJECT MARKETABILITY (Space for comments at the bottom of next page.)

Range of values in the neighborhood is $ _____ to $ _____ .
The subject is an ☐ overimprovement ☐ underimprovement ☐ appropriate improvement for the neighborhood.
Normal marketing time in the area is _____ days.
Marketability of subject property is ☐ Excellent ☐ Good ☐ Fair ☐ Poor
Unit Type: ☐ House ☐ Condo ☐ Townhouse ☐ Muti-family(no. of units _____) ☐ Modular
If condo or other associations exist: Fees are $ _____ /mo. Current? _____ Unpaid how many months? _____
The fee includes: ☐ Pool ☐ Tennis ☐ Insurance ☐ Landscape ☐ Other _____
Association Contact: Name: _____ Phone: _____

III. COMPETITIVE CONTRACT OFFERINGS OR LISTINGS

ITEM	SUBJECT	COMPARABLE NO. 1		COMPARABLE NO. 2		COMPARABLE NO. 3	
Address							
Proximity to Subject							
Current List Price	$	$		$		$	
Original List Price	$	$		$		$	
Current Price/GLA	$	$		$		$	
REO/Corporate Prop?		☐ N ☐ Y		☐ N ☐ Y		☐ N ☐ Y	
Data Source							
VALUE ADJUSTMENTS	DESCRIPTION	DESCRIPTION	+(−) Adjustment	DESCRIPTION	+(−) Adjustment	DESCRIPTION	+(−) Adjustment
Days On Market							
Location							
Site/View/Land Lease							
Design and Appeal							
Quality of Construction							
Age							
Condition/Repairs/Cosmetic							
Systems, Structural Environmental							
Above Grade Room Count	Total ; Bdrms. ; Baths	Total ; Bdrms. ; Baths		Total ; Bdrms. ; Baths		Total ; Bdrms. ; Baths	
Gross Living Area	Sq. Ft.	Sq. Ft.		Sq. Ft.		Sq. Ft.	
Basement & Finished Rooms Below Grade							
Functional Utility							
Heating/Cooling							
Garage/Carport							
Porches, Patios Pools, etc.							
Special Energy Efficient Items							
Fireplace(s)							
Other (e.g. kitchen equip., remodeling)							
Sales or Financing Concessions							
Net Adj. (total)		☒ + ☐ −	$	☒ + ☐ −	$	☒ + ☐ −	$
Indicated Value of Subject		Net _____ % Gross _____ %	$	Net _____ % Gross _____ %	$	Net _____ % Gross _____ %	$

(COMPARABLE ANALYSIS)

BROKER PRICE OPINION (10 CH. B Revised 3/29/96)

BROKER'S PRICE OPINION

FannieMae

IV. MARKETING STRATEGY

Most likely buyer: ☐ Owner occupant ☐ Investor

Planned Marketing Action in addition to cleaning, repairing, signage, MLS and lock box (be specific): _____
_____
_____

Recommended repairs and your estimate of cost by item. Attach addendum if additional space is needed.

_____	$ _____	_____
_____	$ _____	_____
_____	$ _____	_____
_____	$ _____	_____
_____	$ _____	_____
TOTAL REPAIRS	$ _____	

V. COMPETITIVE CLOSED SALES

ITEM	SUBJECT	COMPARABLE NO. 1		COMPARABLE NO. 2		COMPARABLE NO. 3	
Address							
Proximity to Subject							
Sales Price	$	$		$		$	
Current List Price	$	$		$		$	
Sale Price/GLA	$ ⌀	$ ⌀		$ ⌀		$ ⌀	
REO/Corporate Prop?		☐ N ☐ Y		☐ N ☐ Y		☐ N ☐ Y	
Data Source							
VALUE ADJUSTMENTS	DESCRIPTION	DESCRIPTION	+(−) Adjustment	DESCRIPTION	+(−) Adjustment	DESCRIPTION	+(−) Adjustment
Date of Sale/DOM							
Location							
Site/View/Land Lease							
Design and Appeal							
Quality of Construction							
Age							
Condition/Repairs/Cosmetic							
Systems, Structural Environmental							
Above Grade Room Count	Total : Bdrms. : Baths	Total : Bdrms. : Baths		Total : Bdrms. : Baths		Total : Bdrms. : Baths	
Gross Living Area	Sq. Ft.	Sq. Ft.		Sq. Ft.		Sq. Ft.	
Basement & Finished Rooms Below Grade							
Functional Utility							
Heating/Cooling							
Garage/Carport							
Porches, Patios Pools, etc.							
Special Energy Efficient Items							
Fireplace(s)							
Other (e.g. kitchen equip., remodeling)							
Sales or Financing Concessions							
Net Adj. (total)		☒ + ☐ −	$	☒ + ☐ −	$	☒ + ☐ −	$
Indicated Value of Subject			$		$		$

COMPARABLE ANALYSIS

VI. THE MARKET VALUE

must fall within the indicated value of the sales used above.

THE VALUE FOR THE SUBJECT PROPERTY BASED ON 120 DAYS LIST TO CONTRACT IS:

	MARKET VALUE	SUGGESTED LIST PRICE	AVAILABLE FINANCING	BROKER RECOMMENDS MARKETING EITHER
As is	$	$	Conv ☐ FHA/VA ☐ Other ☐	☐ OR
As Repaired	$	$	Conv ☐ FHA/VA ☐ Other ☐	☐

COMMENTS including specific positives on this property and special concerns, if any, such as apparent structural issues, encroachments, easements, water rights, propane, hazardous waste, flood zone, etc. Attach addendum if additional space is needed.

_____
_____
_____
_____
_____

_____   _____
Agent's Signature   Date

BROKER'S PRICE OPINION (10 CH. B Revised 3/29/96)

A. Settlement Statement

U.S. Department of Housing and Urban Development

OMB Approval No. 2502-0265

B. Type of Loan

1. ☐ FHA	2. ☐ FmHA	3. ☐ Conv. Unins.
4. ☐ VA	5. ☑ Conv. Ins.	

6. File Number:
7. Loan Number: FL 082819501
8. Mortgage Insurance Case Number: PMI 8292109643

C. Note: This form is furnished to give you a statement of actual settlement costs. Amounts paid to and by the settlement agent are shown. Items marked "(p.o.c.)" were paid outside the closing; they are shown here for informational purposes and are not included in the totals.

D. Name & Address of Borrower:	E. Name & Address of Seller:	F. Name & Address of Lender:
Charles H. Buyer 5620 Rich Avenue Orlando, FL 32890	Robert D. Default 3345 Costa Rosa Way Tampa, FL 33649	Bank of Florida 2679 Florida Avenue Tampa, FL 33689

G. Property Location:	H. Settlement Agent:	
3345 Costa Rosa Way Tampa, FL 33649	John B. Good	
	Place of Settlement: 2407 Keene Road Tampa, FL 33629	I. Settlement Date: September 5, 2003

J. Summary of Borrower's Transaction		K. Summary of Seller's Transaction	
100. Gross Amount Due From Borrower		**400. Gross Amount Due To Seller**	
101. Contract sales price	90,000	401. Contract sales price	90,000
102. Personal property		402. Personal property	
103. Settlement charges to borrower (line 1400)	4018.15	403.	
104.		404.	
105.		405.	
Adjustments for items paid by seller in advance		**Adjustments for items paid by seller in advance**	
106. City/town taxes to		406. City/town taxes to	
107. County taxes to		407. County taxes to	
108. Assessments to		408. Assessments to	
109.		409.	
110.		410.	
111.		411.	
112.		412.	
120. Gross Amount Due From Borrower	94,018.15	**420. Gross Amount Due To Seller**	
200. Amounts Paid By Or In Behalf Of Borrower		**500. Reductions In Amount Due To Seller**	
201. Deposit or earnest money	500.00	501. Excess deposit (see instructions)	
202. Principal amount of new loan(s)		502. Settlement charges to seller (line 1400)	
203. Existing loan(s) taken subject to		503. Existing loan(s) taken subject to	
204.		504. Payoff of first mortgage loan	90,000
205.		505. Payoff of second mortgage loan	
206.		506.	
207.		507.	
208.		508.	
209.		509.	
Adjustments for items unpaid by seller		**Adjustments for items unpaid by seller**	
210. City/town taxes to		510. City/town taxes to	
211. County taxes to		511. County taxes to	
212. Assessments to		512. Assessments to	
213.		513.	
214.		514.	
215.		515.	
216.		516.	
217.		517.	
218.		518.	
219.		519.	
220. Total Paid By/For Borrower	500.00	**520. Total Reduction Amount Due Seller**	
300. Cash At Settlement From/To Borrower		**600. Cash At Settlement To/From Seller**	
301. Gross Amount due from borrower (line 120)	94,018.15	601. Gross amount due to seller (line 420)	
302. Less amounts paid by/for borrower (line 220)	(500.00)	602. Less reductions in amt. due seller (line 520)	( )
303. Cash ☑ From ☐ To Borrower	93,518.15	603. Cash ☐ To ☑ From Seller	90,000

Section 5 of the Real Estate Settlement Procedures Act (RESPA) requires the following: • HUD must develop a Special Information Booklet to help persons borrowing money to finance the purchase of residential real estate to better understand the nature and costs of real estate settlement services; • Each lender must provide the booklet to all applicants from whom it receives or for whom it prepares a written application to borrow money to finance the purchase of residential real estate; • Lenders must prepare and distribute with the Booklet a Good Faith Estimate of the settlement costs that the borrower is likely to incur in connection with the settlement. These disclosures are manadatory.

Section 4(a) of RESPA mandates that HUD develop and prescribe this standard form to be used at the time of loan settlement to provide full disclosure of all charges imposed upon the borrower and seller. These are third party disclosures that are designed to provide the borrower with pertinent information during the settlement process in order to be a better shopper.

The Public Reporting Burden for this collection of information is estimated to average one hour per response, including the time for reviewing instructions, searching existing data sources, gathering and maintaining the data needed, and completing and reviewing the collection of information.

This agency may not collect this information, and you are not required to complete this form, unless it displays a currently valid OMB control number.

The information requested does not lend itself to confidentiality.

Previous editions are obsolete

L. Settlement Charges

				Paid From Borrowers Funds at Settlement	Paid From Seller's Funds at Settlement
700. Total Sales/Broker's Commission based on price $		@	% =		
Division of Commission (line 700) as follows:					
701. $		to			
702. $		to			
703. Commission paid at Settlement					
704.					
800. Items Payable In Connection With Loan					
801. Loan Origination Fee		%			
802. Loan Discount		%			
803. Appraisal Fee		to			
804. Credit Report		to			
805. Lender's Inspection Fee					
806. Mortgage Insurance Application Fee to					
807. Assumption Fee					
808.					
809.					
810.					
811.					
900. Items Required By Lender To Be Paid In Advance					
901. Interest from	to	@ $	/day		
902. Mortgage Insurance Premium for			months to		
903. Hazard Insurance Premium for			years to		
904.			years to		
905.					
1000. Reserves Deposited With Lender					
1001. Hazard insurance		months @ $	per month		
1002. Mortgage insurance		months @ $	per month		
1003. City property taxes		months @ $	per month		
1004. County property taxes		months @ $	per month	1867.40	
1005. Annual assessments		months @ $	per month		
1006.		months @ $	per month		
1007.		months @ $	per month		
1008.		months @ $	per month		
1100. Title Charges					
1101. Settlement or closing fee		to		275.00	
1102. Abstract or title search		to		150.00	
1103. Title examination		to			
1104. Title insurance binder		to			
1105. Document preparation		to		75.00	
1106. Notary fees		to		17.50	
1107. Attorney's fees		to		250.00	
(includes above items numbers:			)		
1108. Title insurance		to			
(includes above items numbers:			)		
1109. Lender's coverage		$			
1110. Owner's coverage		$		517.50	
1111.					
1112.					
1113.					
1200. Government Recording and Transfer Charges					
1201. Recording fees: Deed $	11.50 ; Mortgage $	; Releases $	11.50	23.00	
1202. City/county tax/stamps: Deed $	180.00 ; Mortgage $			180.00	
1203. State tax/stamps: Deed $	630.00 ; Mortgage $			630.00	
1204.					
1205.					
1300. Additional Settlement Charges					
1301. Survey	to				
1302. Pest inspection to					
1303. Courier Fees				32.75	
1304.					
1305.					
1400. Total Settlement Charges (enter on lines 103, Section J and 502, Section K)				4018.15	

Chapter Thirteen

How To
Fix-Up Pre-Foreclosure Properties
For Maximum Curb Appeal And Resale Value

Your goal during the fix-up is to increase the property's curb and resale value by:
1. Giving the property and grounds an industrial strength cleaning.
2. Applying a cosmetic facelift to the exterior of the property and grounds.
3. Applying a cosmetic facelift to the interior.

Know What You Don't Know About Property Repairs

A word to the wise: If you're thinking about doing the fix-up yourself, first ask yourself this question: Do I have the knowledge, skill, and experience necessary to do a top-notch, professional quality job? Be honest with yourself. I've seen a lot of money wasted by so-called "weekend handymen" who didn't possess the skill levels necessary to achieve a first class job, and had to call in a professional at a great expense to "bail them out" and redo their handiwork. Know your limitations and abide by them. Don't try to save money by doing repairs, which you aren't qualified to do. In other words, know what you don't know about property repairs, and never attempt to "fix stuff" that you know absolutely nothing about, regardless of how many times you've seen Norm fix it on reruns of "This Old House!" The often-heard refrain of, "don't try this at home," should be applicable to all amateurs for any repairs.

Seven Key Elements That Must Be Included In Your Property Fix-Up Plan

The trick to having a fast property fix-up that's on schedule and within budget is to be well organized. In order to do this, you must make certain to include the following seven key elements in your property fix-up plan:

1. **Budget:** Establish a bottom-line budget before you start the job.
2. **Total job cost estimate:** Estimate to within five percent how much the total fix-up is going to cost.
3. **Labor:** If you don't have the knowledge, experience, and time to do a first class professional looking job, hire competent tradesmen and contractors to do it for you.
4. **Job supervision:** If you don't have the knowledge and time to supervise the job yourself, hire a competent professional to do it for you.
5. **Quality control:** Have all of the completed work inspected to make certain that is has been done in a professional manner in accordance with acceptable construction methods and building codes.
6. **Work schedule:** Set a coordinated work schedule to complete the entire job.
7. **Completion date:** Put completion dates in all your contracts and hold everyone accountable.

How To Avoid Being Ripped-Off By Unscrupulous Repairmen And Contractors

Here are three ways that you can avoid being ripped of by the many unscrupulous repairmen, tradesmen and contractors who make a living taking real estate investors "to-the-cleaners" on a regular basis:
1. Hire only properly licensed and insured repairmen, tradesmen and contractors.
2. Require written estimates for all jobs.
3. Require that everyone who provides labor and materials on your job sign your state's version of a waiver and release of lien upon final payment form.

How To Hire Only Properly Licensed And Insured Repairmen And Contractors

In order to avoid being duped into hiring one of the numerous unlicensed and uninsured crooks masquerading as legitimate repairmen and contractors, you must follow these eight steps to weed out the phonies, fakes and frauds:

Step #1: Require that all repairmen and contractors provide copies of their license or certificate of competency, occupational license, workers' compensation insurance certificate, workers' compensation exemption certificate for sole employees, general liability insurance certificate and automobile liability insurance certificate.
Step #2: Require that all repairmen and contractors provide four verifiable customer references.
Step #3: Contact all of the customer references provided and ask them if they would hire the repairman or contractor again.
Step #4: Conduct an online search of your state's contractor license database to verify that the contractor has a valid license.
Step #5: Contact all of the insurers listed on the insurance certificates to verify that the policies are valid and in effect.
Step #6: Contact your local city and county building departments to check if there's a history of complaints against the repairman or contractor.
Step #7: Contact your local Better Business Bureau to check if there's a history of complaints against the repairman or contractor.
Step #8: Log onto your state attorney general's consumer investigations Web page to check if the repairman or contractor is under investigation.

How To Find Competent Professional Tradesmen And Contractors

How do you find competent professional tradesmen and contractors? Start by looking on the Internet and in your local newspaper under the professional services section. Or, better yet, visit construction job sites and ask tradesmen if they're interested in "side-work." In most cases, they will be. Ask them for references from people they have done work for. Also, try to see previous examples of their work. A little investigative work on your part could pay handsome dividends, especially if it helps you to avoid being stuck with a less than professional looking job. I've had good luck hiring retired tradesmen who are looking for part-time employment.

Require Written Estimates For All Jobs

In order to avoid being ripped off by unscrupulous repairmen and contractors, require written estimates that include the following information:
1. Detailed description of the scope of all work to be performed on the job to include cleanup.
2. Detailed work schedule with commencement and completion dates.
3. Specifications for all building materials to be used on the job.
4. Listing of all building permits required to perform the job.
5. Detailed payment schedule outlining the amount and time when payments are to be made.
6. Warranties covering workmanship and building materials used on the job.

What You Need To Know About Your State's Construction Lien Law

You need to know that under most state construction lien laws, anyone who provides a service, labor or materials for the improvement of real property has a right to file a lien against the property for nonpayment. Furthermore, if you do pay a contractor for a job, and the contractor fails to pay the subcontractors who supplied the labor and the materialmen who supplied the materials, you're still financially responsible for paying them even though you've paid the contractor in full. In other words, you could end up paying for a job twice if you don't have legal proof that everyone was paid in full.

Require Everyone Who Works Or Supplies Materials To Sign A Release Of Lien

In order to avoid paying for a job twice, require that everyone who works or supplies materials on your job sign a Waiver And Release Of Lien Upon Final Payment when they're paid. This way, you'll have legal proof that everyone connected to your property fix-up was paid in full.

Building And Repair Cost Calculators Online

The following Web sites have building and repair cost calculators online that you can use to get a "ballpark" figure on what various repairs in your area should cost:
Construction Cost Calculator
www.get-a-quote.net
Construction Material Calculators
www.constructionworkcenter.com/calculators.html
Building Cost Calculator
www.nt.receptive.com/rsmeans/calculator

Give The Property An Industrial Strength Cleaning

The first step in the property fix-up phase is to thoroughly clean the property's exterior to include the roof and all walkways and parking areas. You can apply an industrial strength cleaning to any type of property by using a pressure washer with a minimum capacity of 3500 PSI at 3.5 GPM. Pressure washing will remove all dirt, grime, soot, oils, and other pollutants from all exterior surfaces. I recommend that you hire the services of a competent professional pressure washing service that uses state-of-the-art equipment and the proper chemicals. The main objective in having your property's exterior thoroughly washed is to be able to see what is beneath the last five year's worth of dirt, filth, and grime. It's really amazing what a professional pressure washing can do to a property's appearance. Plus, pressure washing eliminates a lot of labor-intensive work such as scraping paint. In most cases, the only things necessary prior to applying the finishing coat of exterior paint will be caulking and priming the surfaces. Lastly, a thorough pressure washing will expose any rotted wood and other building materials needing replacement.

Always Complete The Exterior Facelift First

Rule number one in the fix-up of any pre-foreclosure property is to always complete the exterior "facelift" first. This way, the property looks enticing from the curb and helps to lure potential buyers inside for a further look.

Don't Scrimp On Paint

Don't scrimp on the quality of paint or the cost of a quality paint job. An amateurish looking paint job done by an inexperienced painter with cheap paint, sticks out like a sore thumb, while a professional looking paint job will literally add thousands of dollars to a property's resale value. Fact is, there's no greater return on investment than the increased value brought by a top quality, professional looking exterior and interior paint job. I am constantly amazed at how a good quality paint job can drastically upgrade the appearance and resale value of any property.

Choose An Exterior Color Scheme That Enhances Your Property's Curb Appeal

It's extremely important that you choose an exterior paint color scheme that will enhance your property's curb appeal. I use a three-color exterior paint scheme that my wife, Barbara, came up with in 1995. It incorporates three "tropical colors" that people generally associate with Florida. For example, I paint the body of the building one color, the fascia and exterior doors one color and the drip edge around the roof and window shutters one color. Go to paint related Web sites online or visit your local paint store for suggestions on the exterior color schemes that will best accentuate your property's character and charm.

Select An Interior Color Scheme That Uses Neutral Colors

The interior walls and ceilings should be painted in light neutral colors, using quality interior flat latex paint. The interior trim and doors should be painted with latex semi-gloss enamel paint. For example, I use a two-color interior color scheme: flat white paint on walls and ceilings and antique white semi-gloss on trim and doors. Please keep in mind that a professional interior paint job using quality paint will enhance a rental unit's appearance and increase the property's resale value, while a shoddy paint job using cheap paint will detract from a rental unit's appearance and do nothing to contribute to the property's resale value!

Apply Textured Coatings To Rough Interior Wall And Ceiling Surfaces

You can avoid the cost of replacing interior walls and ceilings that have rough surfaces by applying a textured coating to them. A professional looking texture job will greatly enhance the appearance of your "problem walls and ceilings." In most cases, the best and least expensive texture to use is premixed joint compound. Joint compound will bond to most wall and ceiling surfaces such as drywall, lath and plaster. And, pre-mixed joint compound is less expensive and easier to apply than conventional plaster mixes.

My Property Fix-Up Motto Has Always Been Clean, Repair Or Replace As Needed

Being a parsimonious Yankee from New Hampshire, my property fix-up motto has always been clean, repair or replace as needed. In other words, first try cleaning it, and if that doesn't do the trick, try repairing, and if that doesn't work replace it with a pre-owned replacement from a reputable source. The following is a listing of items that must be cleaned, patched, repaired or replaced when fixing up a pre-foreclosure property:
1. **Walkways and parking areas.** Clean, repair, patch and seal all walkways and parking areas as needed.
2. **Mailboxes.** Clean, repair or replace all mailboxes as needed.
3. **Exterior doors.** Clean, repair or replace all exterior doors, hardware and locksets as needed.
4. **Windows.** Clean, repair or replace window frames, glass and locks as needed.
5. **Exterior lighting.** Clean, repair or replace all exterior light fixtures and bulbs as needed.
6. **Interior doors.** Clean, repair or replace all interior doors, hardware and locksets as needed.
7. **Kitchen cabinets.** Clean, repair or replace all cabinet doors, hardware and countertops as needed.
8. **Interior lighting.** Clean, repair or replace all interior light fixtures and bulbs as needed.
9. **Plumbing fixtures.** Clean, repair, or replace all sinks, tubs, showers, faucets, commodes and vanities as needed.
10. **Heating and cooling systems.** Clean, repair or replace all heating and cooling systems as needed.
11. **Floor coverings:** Clean, repair or replace all carpets and floor coverings as needed.
12. **Exterior and interior paint.** Clean, prepare and paint all exterior and interior surfaces.
13. **Landscaping.** Prune, cut, trim and mow the property's landscaping and lawn as needed.
14. **Gutters and downspouts.** Clean, repair or replace all gutters and downspouts as needed.
15. **Roofs.** Clean, repair or replace as needed.

Conduct Final Walk-Through Inspections Before Making The Final Payments

Lastly, prior to making any final payments to tradesmen and contractors, do a walk-through inspection of the property to determine if all work has been satisfactorily completed. In doing your walk-through, check the quality of the materials and workmanship. Make lists of all the discrepancies you find during your walk-through and give them to each applicable contractor or tradesmen to correct. In doing this, be fair and realistic, but don't let anyone take unfair advantage of you. When making your final payments, be certain you get a release of lien form signed by each contractor or tradesmen which states that they've been paid in full for all labor and materials used on your property.

Don't Get Carried Away During The Fix-Up

Lastly, please don't get carried away during the fix-up and do foolish things like putting up expensive vertical blinds, installing expensive floor coverings, or mirroring bedroom ceilings. When doing a cosmetic facelift on a pre-foreclosure property, never lose sight of your fix-up objective, which should always be to maximize the property's curb appeal and resale by giving it an industrial cleaning and cosmetic facelift. Nothing more.

Best To Keep Track Of Your Property Repair Expenses On A Daily Basis

The best way to keep track of your pre-foreclosure property repair costs so that you stay on budget is to use a daily repair cost worksheet like the sample copy below to record both material and labor costs:

Sample Daily Repair Cost Worksheet

Date	Material Costs	Labor Costs	Miscellaneous	Total Cost

Chapter Fourteen

How To Package, Market And Resell Pre-Foreclosure Properties For Maximum Profit

It should come as no surprise to most people, that there's a direct correlation between how well a property is marketed and how fast it sells. Fact is, properties that are properly packaged and advertised to the potential buyers, almost always sell much faster than properties that are poorly advertised. Yet, I'm constantly amazed at the number of investors, whose idea of marketing a property, consists of placing a crude looking for sale sign on their property and then waiting by the telephone, for the "thundering herd" of would-be buyers, to call them. I'm also surprised whenever an investor is duped into signing an exclusive right-to-sell listing agreement with a real estate broker. Especially when the decision to do so, was based solely on unsupported claims the broker made, about how fast they could sell the property. I don't know about you, but I sure as heck don't want to take a hands-off marketing approach and rely on homemade for sale signs or dishonest real estate brokers, to resell my property. As far as I'm concerned, investors in today's competitive real estate market must take an active, hands-on, proactive marketing approach, in order to quickly resell pre-foreclosure properties--within thirty to sixty days--for maximum profit. However, in order to do this, you must first know how to:
1. Calculate the resale value of a pre-foreclosure property.
2. Gauge local real estate market conditions.
3. Package pre-foreclosure properties to highlight their best features.
4. Use an outgoing message on your telephone answering machine to advertise property.
5. Advertise pre-foreclosure properties on the Internet to prospective buyers worldwide.
6. Have real estate brokers help you sell your property, without ever signing a listing agreement.
7. Send property fact sheets to potential buyers by e-mail.
5. Establish a network of potential buyers.
6. Assign or sell your purchase agreements to third parties.

How To Calculate The Resale Value Of A Pre-Foreclosure Property

The first step in packaging a pre-foreclosure property for resale is to determine its value, based on the sale of comparable properties within the same area. To do this, use the same step-by-step instructions that are outlined in chapter nine, to calculate a pre-foreclosure property's current market value. Next, have three residential real estate agents give you listing presentations, to see what they think your property's resale value is. Then compare the resale value that each real estate agent gave you, with the resale value that you calculated. Once you've done this, you should have a good idea of what the property's resale value is. A word of caution: when calculating a pre-foreclosure property's resale value, don't get greedy. In other words, don't try and suck every last dime out of the deal. Instead, price your property at least five percent below its fair market value. Also, when you calculate a property's resale price, be sure to include the cost of:
1. Searching for the property.
2. Acquiring the property.
3. Putting the property in a marketable resale condition.
4. Marketing the property for resale.
5. Your time spent on the transaction.

Local Real Estate Market And Economic Conditions Effect Real Estate Sales

It should be a no-brainer that local real estate market and economic conditions have a direct effect on real estate sales. For example, in real estate markets that are so-called "buyer's markets," there are more properties for sale, than qualified buyers to buy them. This problem brings us back to the simplest concept of economics 101, supply and demand. The supply, the number of properties for sale, is greater than the demand, the number of qualified buyers ready, willing and able to buy. When supply is greater than demand, two things generally happen. Sales' prices decrease, and the amount of time it takes to sell a property, increases. To illustrate, under what would be considered "normal" market conditions, a "fast" sale, is generally considered to be any sale taking less than sixty days. However, during uncertain economic conditions, a "fast" sale could be considered any sale taking less than one hundred and twenty days. Another factor, which contributes to slower sales during uncertain economic conditions, is buyers' reluctance or unwillingness to commit to large purchases such as real estate. What happens, is that a wait-and-see attitude prevails among many qualified buyers, who may actually be in the market to buy, but who are reluctant to invest, because of real or perceived fears they may have about the future of the economy.

Qualified Buyers Are Hard To Find In Most Real Estate Markets Today

In most real estate markets today, it's not easy to find qualified buyers. In other words, responsible, employed adults, with the income, down payment, creditworthiness, and debt-to-income ratios, that are necessary to assume an existing loan, or obtain a new loan from an institutional lender. Experience has shown me that roughly fifty percent of all prospective buyers, are "credit-challenged," and can't qualify for any type of loan, other than from a pawn shop, and maybe not even then. The main reasons for this are insufficient income and a bad credit history that often includes, a previous personal bankruptcy or foreclosure. Or, if a potential buyer does qualify for a loan, they don't have the down payment necessary to buy the property. Also, I've found many qualified buyers, usually prefer to buy new homes directly from builders, who are willing to make concessions, that an individual selling an existing house, can't afford to make.

You Must Be Realistic And Persistent When Reselling Pre-Foreclosure Properties

In order to quickly resell your pre-foreclosure properties within thirty to sixty days, you must be realistic and above all, persistent. Your property must have a realistic sale price that's based on what comparable properties are selling for. But more importantly, you must be consistently persistent. This means following up on every prospective buyer who inquires about your property for sale. You must do this, in order to try and get them to view your property and then make an offer. Persistence means knowing that every "no" that you hear, takes you one step closer to a "yes."

Compile A Property Information Sheet Listing All Of Your Property's Features

I recommend that you do what I always do and compile a comprehensive property information sheet that lists all of the property's features. Your property information sheet should contain the following information:
1. Your name, Web site address, e-mail address and telephone number.
2. The street address of the property being sold.
3. The asking price, sale terms and existing loan information.
4. The year the property was built along with the type of construction and architectural style.
5. The square footage of living space and the number of bedrooms and bathrooms.
6. Descriptions of the living room, dining room, family room, den, carport, utility room, garage, basement, and any other rooms.
7. The type of heating and air conditioning system.
8. Descriptions of the fenced-in yard, sprinkler system, security system, swimming pool, spa, patio, deck, landscaping and other special features about the property.

Package Pre-Foreclosure Properties To Highlight Their Best Features

How much you're able to resell your pre-foreclosure property for is tied directly to how well you're able to package the property. By packaging a property, I mean to present the property to buyers in a way that fully highlights its best features. Make sure you fully highlight the following four features when preparing your pre-foreclosure property package:
1. Property's geographical location to include any special features or benefits about the area and neighborhood.
2. Size and shape of the property to include any unique architectural features.
3. Nearby sources of public transportation, employment, shopping, schools, recreation and healthcare facilities.
4. Special features and amenities about the property and grounds to include lush landscaping, large shade trees, fenced yard and detached home office.

The Three Best Methods To Market Pre-Foreclosure Properties Online

I've found the following three methods to be the best ways to market pre-foreclosure properties online, to potential buyers worldwide:
1. Property for sale Web pages.
2. Property for sale ads online.
3. Property e-mail fact sheets.

Use The Internet To Market Your Pre-Foreclosure Properties Globally

The key to quickly reselling your pre-foreclosure properties is to market them to the largest possible number of potential buyers. In today's "wired world," this includes the global audience of potential buyers that are available online via the World Wide Web. Fact is, American real estate attracts investors from around the globe. For example, here in Central Florida, people from the United Kingdom, Germany, The Netherlands, Canada and Spain are continually investing in residential and commercial real estate. You also need to know that many European investors are "cash buyers," who don't have to play the "mortgage loan disqualification game" with lenders, in order to buy property! As far as I'm concerned, it's absolutely imperative that you use the Internet to tap into the global real estate marketplace, and expose your pre-foreclosure properties to prospective buyers worldwide.

Create A Property For Sale Web Page To Advertise Your Properties Online

If you already have an existing Web site, all you'll have to do is to create a property for sale Web page or pages to advertise your pre-foreclosure properties for sale online. To see an example, log onto www.homeequitiescorp.com, and click on the Property For Sale button. I recommend that you include the following information on your property for sale Web page:
1. Property photograph.
2. Property location map.
3. Property site plan.
4. Property features.
5. Property sale price and terms.

Mapping Information Available Online

The following is a listing of Web sites which provide online location maps and driving directions, that you can use on your property for sale Web page:
MapQuest
www.mapquest.com
MapBlast
www.mapblast.com
Maptech
www.mapserver.maptech.com
Expedia
www.expedia.com
Topozone
www.tpozone.com
Yahoo Maps
www.maps.yahoo.com
Maps
www.maps.com

Use URL Forwarding For Property For Sale Domain Names

First and foremost, use what I commonly refer to as the "great equalizer"--the Internet--to market your pre-foreclosure properties online. The most efficient way that I know to do this is by having a property for sale Web page on your Web site, that uses URL forwarding for a "property for sale" domain name. If you already have an existing Web site online, for an annual fee of around $50, you can have your property for sale domain name forwarded to a specific Web page on your Web site. For example, when you use URL forwarding, or "domain redirection," you can link your property for sale domain name directly to a property for sale Web page on your existing Web site. This way, you avoid the cost and aggravation of building an entirely new Web site, for your property for sale domain name. For example, if you were reselling pre-foreclosure properties in Glendale, California, you could register the domain name, www.glendalehomesforsale.com, to market your properties to potential buyers worldwide, via the Internet. Whenever this domain name is typed into a search engine, the URL would automatically be forwarded to an existing Web site, which is the destination domain.

Have Visitors To Your Web Site Complete A Buyer E-Mail Notification Form

On the Home Equities Corp Property For Sale Web page, there's a Buyer E-Mail Notification Form, that Web site visitors can complete to submit their name and e-mail address in order to be notified by e-mail, when there's a property for sale. I recommend that you do the same thing on your Web site, so that you can compile a list of potential buyers, who can be notified by e-mail, when you have a pre-foreclosure property for sale.

What To Include In Your Pre-Foreclosure Property For Sale E-Mail Fact Sheet

When notifying potential buyers via e-mail, about a pre-foreclosure property that you have for sale, send them a property fact sheet that includes the following information:
1. Property address.
2. Description of the property.
3. Sale price and terms.
4. Location map of the property.
5. Driving directions to the property.

Place Classified Ads In Local Newspapers

In addition to using property for sale Web pages, online advertising, and e-mail property fact sheets to market your pre-foreclosure properties, place classified ads in local daily and weekly newspapers like the ad below, that have your Web site address, e-mail address and telephone number.

Homes For Sale
www.glendalehomesforsale.com
sales@glendalehomesforsale.com
(818) 123-4567

Use "Qualifiers" In Your Classified Ads

The "buyer-qualifying" process begins with your classified ad copy. When writing ads, you want to include as many "qualifiers" such as the down payment, and total monthly payment amount in the ad's headline and body copy. For example, suppose you have a pre-foreclosure property for sale requiring a $5,000 down payment, with seller financing, via a wraparound mortgage or all-inclusive deed of trust, to buyers with good credit, and the income to pay $980 a month in loan payments. To advertise your house using these qualifiers, your ad would read as follows:

> **$5,000 Moves You In!**
> **Seller Will Finance With Good Credit**
> **Only $980 Total Monthly Payment**
> **Call (818) 123-4567 For Details**

This way, potential buyers reading the ad will be able to quickly determine three things. They need $5,000 for the down payment, a good credit rating in order to get seller financing, and the monthly income necessary to make a $980 monthly loan payment. In most cases, people who don't meet any of these three qualifications will not call.

Place A Professional Looking For Sale Sign On The Property

The next marketing tool that you must use to advertise your pre-foreclosure property for sale, is a professional looking for sale sign. The sign by itself may not sell the property, but it will let people know that the property is for sale.

Use Word-Of-Mouth Advertising To Help Sell Your Pre-Foreclosure Properties

Word-of-mouth advertising is probably the most effective form of advertising. Talk to a lot of people. Tell them that you have property for sale. In addition to talking to people, always be sure to pass out and exchange business cards. This will help you accumulate names of potential buyers. Word of mouth advertising is very effective, because it can make large numbers of people aware of your name and properties.

Record An Outgoing Message On Your Telephone Answering Machine

In conjunction with your property for sale Web page, online advertising, classified advertising and for sale sign, record a detailed outgoing telephone message on your telephone answering machine, which explains in detail, the property's features, location, sale price, sale terms and directions to the property. Below is a copy of an outgoing telephone message that I've successfully used to sell pre-foreclosure properties:

Sample Outgoing Telephone Message

You've reached the sales office of Home Equities Corp. Thank you for calling about the home we have located at 4429 Park Drive in Tampa as advertised in today's Tampa Tribune. 4429 Park Drive is approximately three blocks south of Kern Blvd and two blocks east of Bay View Drive. This charming home is block construction, and only eight years young. It has three bedrooms and two bathrooms, with a total living space of fourteen hundred square feet. This house comes complete with a frost-free refrigerator, range, ceiling fans, blinds and drapes, wall-to-wall carpeting, central heat and air, and an oversized two-car garage. The lot is seventy feet wide by one hundred twenty feet deep. There's fencing and a large utility shed in the backyard. This home is priced at $145,000 for a fast sale, as its sale price, is below the sale prices of comparable neighboring homes that have recently been sold!

Please note that the sellers are unable to provide any type of owner financing and that whomever buys this home, must be able to obtain a mortgage loan in the $145,000 price range, in order to finance the purchase. This home is being shown by appointment only to serious homebuyers, who have been pre-approved by a Florida licensed mortgage lender for a mortgage loan in the $145,000 price range. Please call back and leave a message, if you would like to set up an appointment to see this quaint home, after you have driven by it.

Four Qualifying Questions That You Must Ask Potential Buyers

The four main qualifying questions, that you must ask when you meet with potential buyers, are:
1. Do you currently have the cash on hand to pay the down payment and closing costs?
2. Do you have the verifiable income necessary to pay the monthly loan payments?
3. Do you have the creditworthiness necessary to qualify for a mortgage or deed of trust loan?
4. Are you able to close on the purchase of the property within the next thirty days?

Asking these four qualifying questions, during your initial meeting with potential buyers, helps to quickly determine, if they're really serious buyers, who can afford to buy the property that you're selling, or just "lookers," out to waste your valuable time. Potential buyers who refuse to answer any one of these four questions aren't worth pursuing!

How To Work With Real Estate Brokers Without Signing A Listing Agreement

If you want local real estate brokers to show their clients your pre-foreclosure properties, without your having to sign an exclusive listing agreement, have them sign a participating broker agreement, like the sample copy below. Under a properly written participating broker agreement, you would only pay a sales commission, when a broker's registered prospect, bought the property. In the meantime, you avoid having your property "tied-up," by an exclusive listing agreement.

Sample Participating Broker Agreement

This agreement made this nineteenth day of August 2003 between David D. Jones, known hereinafter as the Seller and Douglas Avery known hereinafter as the Broker. Broker holds a valid real estate broker's license, license number 568976, issued by the state of Florida.

Seller agrees to pay the Broker a brokerage commission, equal to three percent of the purchase price and payable at the time of the closing, when the Broker's prospect purchases the Seller's property, under the following conditions:

1. Participating Broker must register the Broker's prospects with the Seller, by mailing, on the Broker's company stationery, the Broker's prospect's name, signed by the Broker and the Broker's prospect. If the Broker fails to register prospects with the Seller, as set forth, no commission will be paid to the Broker. No oral registrations of the Broker's prospects with the Seller will be accepted.

2. Participating Broker may serve only as a broker representing prospects and not as a principal, lender, or other financial participant in the purchase of the Seller's property. No commission shall be paid to any Broker participating as a buyer of the Seller's property.

3. Neither participating Broker nor any principal thereof, licensed salesperson associated therewith, nor any employee or licensee thereof, is, or will be, a principal or financial participant with or lender to, any buyer of the Seller's property.

IN WITNESS WHEREOF, Seller and Broker have set their hands the date aforesaid.

Seller   Broker
David D. Jones   Douglas Avery

How To Make Money As A Pre-Foreclosure Property Wholesaler

You can make money as a pre-foreclosure property wholesaler, simply by finding, researching, negotiating, and placing pre-foreclosure properties under contract, in effect, controlling them for immediate resale to a network of "retail" buyers. Many busy career professionals, such as doctors, dentists, attorneys, accountants, small business owners, and other individuals with relatively high incomes, are on the lookout for bargain-priced properties that they can add to their portfolios, or upgrade and sell. In any market, you can always find a large group of investors, both active and armchair types, who are looking for properties, which they can rent out or resell for a profit. However, heavy professional demand, usually prevents such people from having the time, desire, knowledge, skills, and experience necessary to find and negotiate bargain purchases. They want the profits that come with the investments, but they depend upon wholesalers to find bargain priced properties. That's where you, as a "pre-foreclosure property wholesaler," can make money, by finding, researching, negotiating, and putting pre-foreclosure properties under contract. You then sell, that is assign, your purchase agreements to investors and other buyers, in order to make your profit. Once your network of buyers is set up, you'll be in a position to sell your purchase agreements, on the same day that you sign them. This strategy has one very special advantage: it greatly reduces your risks and financial liability. That's because, your investment in any purchase agreement, should never consist of more than a $500 earnest money deposit, a $125 title report and a property appraisal report costing between $350 to $500. And if you use the earnest money deposit clause that's contained in the sample purchase agreement in chapter two, your financial liability in any purchase agreement, would be limited to the forfeiture of your earnest money deposit, as liquidated damages and nothing more.

Price Your Purchase Agreements For A Fast Sale

Don't get greedy when trying to sell your purchase agreements. Instead, do what I do and price your agreements for a fast sale. I recommend that you sell your pre-foreclosure property purchase agreements for right around five percent of the property's current market value. For example, I would sell a purchase agreement on a property under contract for $130,000 and with a current market value of $ 165,000, for $8,000 ($165,000 multiplied by five percent equals $8250).

How To Sell Your Purchase Agreements To Third Parties

What you're really selling, when you sell your purchase agreement, is your exclusive right to buy a property under contract, for a specific purchase price, within a certain period of time. In other words, if someone wants to buy a property that you control with a purchase agreement, they must buy it from you. When you sell a purchase agreement to a third party, you transfer the ownership of the purchase agreement through an assignment of real estate purchase agreement, like the sample copy on the following page. To do this, you and the party buying your purchase agreement, would sign an assignment of real estate purchase agreement, in the presence of a notary public, in which you would assign, or sell all of your rights and interests in the purchase agreement.

Sample Assignment Of Real Estate Purchase Agreement

This agreement made this tenth day of September 2003, between David D. Jones, known hereinafter as the Assignor, and Donald S. Reed, known hereinafter as the Assignee. Assignor and Assignee hereby agree as follows:

In return for the consideration set forth in this agreement, Assignor hereby assigns, sells, and transfers all of Assignor's title and interest in and rights under, the attached agreement entitled, "Purchase Agreement," dated thirteen August, 2003, hereinafter referred to as the "Agreement," executed by John Q. Burns as Seller and by David D. Jones as Buyer, for the purchase of said property known as 4899 Crenshaw Street, Tampa, Florida 33690, and legally described as Lot 34, Block17 of the Elliot and Harrison Subdivision, according to map or plat thereof, as recorded in Plat Book 37, Page 79, of the public records of Hillsborough County, Florida.

By accepting this assignment, Assignee agrees to undertake and perform the obligations imposed on Assignor, as buyer, under the aforementioned Agreement. Assignee accepts this assignment subject to all of the terms and conditions contained in the Agreement, or imposed by law. A copy of the Agreement is attached hereto, as Exhibit "A" and incorporated herein, as if fully set forth herein.

It is hereby agreed, that the obligations of both Assignor and Assignee, hereunder, are not contingent upon the recordation of a deed, or other completion of the purchase of the property, under the Agreement. It is the sole responsibility of Assignee, to seek legal or other relief, in the event that the agreement is not performed, as a result of the act or omission of any other party to the Agreement.

In return for the rights assigned by Assignor herein, Assignee hereby agrees to pay Assignor the sum of five thousand five hundred dollars.

All of the provisions of this assignment of purchase agreement, shall extend to, bind, and inure to the benefit of heirs, executors, personal representatives, successors, and assigns of Assignor and Assignee.

IN WITNESS WHEREOF, Assignor and Assignee have set their hands the date aforesaid.

David D. Jones
Assignor
Robert B. Big
Witness

Donald S. Reed
Assignee
Sally M. Little
Witness

What You Must Know About The Vacancy Exclusion Clause In Insurance Policies

As a pre-foreclosure property investor, you must know that virtually all property and casualty insurance policies, contain what's called a vacancy exclusion clause, that excludes coverage for properties, that have been vacant for thirty to sixty days. Each insurance carrier has their own vacancy exclusion period, that's supposed to be in accordance with state insurance statutes. For example, most insurance policies generally have a vacancy exclusion period of thirty-days. This means that the insurer couldn't be held liable, for any losses that occur to a property that has been vacant for longer than thirty days. This vacancy exclusion clause is important to pre-foreclosure property investors, because it usually takes from thirty to one hundred and twenty days to sell a property. In the meantime, the property is excluded from insurance coverage, which means that the property owner has violated the terms of their mortgage or deed of trust loan, by failing to carry adequate insurance coverage. Plus, the investor risks losing all of their equity, if the property were to become a total loss while vacant and waiting to be sold.

Know How Income From The Sale Of A Pre-Foreclosure Property Is Taxed

You must know how income from the sale of a pre-foreclosure property is taxed, so that you can structure a "tax efficient sale," that allows you to minimize the amount of income tax that you pay from the resale of your pre-foreclosure property. I recommend that you hire an honest, competent tax professional, who specializes in real estate, to help you with tax planning, so that your resale profits, aren't used to pay income taxes.

Internal Revenue Service Publications

You can order the two Internal Revenue Service publications that are listed below, by logging onto www.irs.gov/forms/pubs.html:
1. Publication 537, *Installment Sales*.
2. Publication 946, *How To Depreciate Property*.

Tax Information Online

The following Web Sites provide tax information online:
Internal Revenue Service
www.irs.gov
Internal Revenue Code And Tax Regulations Online
www.tax.cchgroup.com/freecoderegs
Revenue Ruling Bulletins
www.irs.gov/bus_info/bullet.html

Use The *U.S. Master Tax Guide* As Your Tax Reference Guide

Lastly, I highly recommend that you use the, *U.S. Master Tax Guide* as your tax reference guide. It's published annually by the Commerce Clearinghouse and available online at:
Commerce Clearinghouse
wwwtax.cchgroup.com

Real Estate Investor Resources Online

I divide the real estate investment business into BTI--Before the Internet and ATI--After the Internet. In fact, I consider the Internet to be the "great equalizer!" That's because, before the Internet became available to the general public, the average individual real estate investor had no way to readily access public property ownership records, and a myriad of other essential real estate related records. However, now anyone with a computer and an Internet connection, who knows where to look, can gain access to the same information that Fortune 500 companies use to make business decisions. The following is a listing of real estate related Web sites, that every serious pre-foreclosure property investor must have bookmarked on their personal computer:

Internet Search Engines

Google
www.google.com
Lycos
www.lycos.com
Yahoo
www.yahoo.com
AltaVista
www.altavista.com
Vivisimo
www.vivisimo.com
Excite
www.excite.com
AllTheWeb
www.alltheweb.com
Teoma
www.teoma.com

Foreclosure Reporting Services Online

Foreclosure Access
www.foreclosureaccess.com
PropertyTrac
www.propertytrac.com
Foreclosure Data NW
www.foreclosuredatanw.com
Information Resource Service
www.irsfl.com
New York Foreclosures
www.newyorkforeclosures.com
REDLOC
www.redloc.com
ForeclosureTrac
www.foreclosuretrac.com

Bates Foreclosure Report
www.brucebates.com
Foreclosure Reporting Service
www.foreclosure-report.com
Foreclosure Report
www.foreclosurereport.com
Real Data Corp
www.real-data.com
Midwest Foreclosures
www.midwestforeclosures.com
Foreclosure Listing Service
www.foreclosehouston.com
Foreclosure Disclosure Weekly
www.foreclosuredisclosure.com
RETRAN
www.retran.net
County Records Research
www.countyrecordsresearch.com

Property Records Information Online

Real Estate Public Records
www.real-estate-public-records.com
Search Systems
www.searchsystems.net
Tax Assessor Database
www.pubweb.acns.nwu.edu/~cap440/assess.html
Public Records Online
www.netronline.com/public_records.htm
National Association Of Counties
www.naco.org/counties/counties
Public Records USA
www.factfind.com/public.htm
International Association of Assessing Officers
www.iaao.org/1234.html
Public Records Research System
www.brbpub.com

Where To Search For People Online

Internet Address Finder
www.iaf.net
Switchboard
www.switchboard.com
Skipease
www.skipease.com
Social Security Administration Death Index
www.ancestry.com/search/rectype/vital/ssdi/main.htm

Street Address Information
www.melissadata.com/lookups/index.htm
Reverse Telephone Directory
www.reversephonedirectory.com

Crime Information Online

Crime.com
www.crime.com/info/crime_stats/crime_stats.html
Neighborhood crime check
www.apbnews.com/resourcecenter/datacenter/index.html
Nationwide sex registry
www.crimetime.com/bbosex.htm

Environmental Hazardous Waste Information Online

EPA superfund hazardous waste site search
www.epa.gov/superfund/sites/query/basic.htm
Environmental hazards zip code search
www.scorecard.org
EPA Enviromapper zip code search
www.epa.gov/cgi-bin/enviro/em/empact/getZipCode.cgi?appl=empact&info=zipcode
HUD environmental maps
www.hud.gov/offices/cio/emaps/index.cfm

Demographic Information Online

FFIEC Geocoding System
www.ffiec.gov/geocode/default.htm
U.S. Census Bureau FactFinder
www.factfinder.census.gov/servlet/BasicFactsServlet
U.S. Census Bureau Gazetteer
www.census.gov/cgi-bin/gazetteer
U.S. Census Bureau QuickFacts
www.quickfacts.census.gov/qfd/index.html

Maps Online

MapQuest
www.mapquest.com
MapBlast
www.mapblast.com
Maptech
www.mapserver.maptech.com
Expedia
www.expedia.com

Topozone
www.tpozone.com
Yahoo Maps
www.maps.yahoo.com
Maps
www.maps.com

Title Insurance Information Online

American Land Title Association
www.alta.org
TitleWeb
www.titleweb.com
Old Republic National Title Insurance Company
www.orlink.oldrepnatl.com/index.htm
Stewart Title Insurance Company
www.stewart.com
Chicago Title Insurance Company
www.ctic.com
Fidelity National Title Insurance Company
www.fntic.com
First American Title Insurance Company
www.firstam.com/fatic/html/about/site-map.html
Lawyers Title Insurance Corporation
www.landam.com/subsidiaries/LTIC/index.asp

Attorney Locator Services Online

Martindale Hubbell Lawyer Locator
www.martindale.com/locator/home.html
Findlaw
www.findlaw.com/14firms
Lawyers
www.lawyers.com

Comparable Property Sales Data Online

DataQuick
www.dataquick.com
domania
www.domania.com
HomeGain
www.homegain.com
REAL-COMP
www.real-comp.com
HomeRadar
www.homeradar.com

Property Replacement Cost Information Online

Marshall & Swift
www.marshallswift.com
Craftsman Book Company
www.craftsman-book.com
R.S. Means Company
www.rsmeans.com
Construction Cost Calculator
www.get-a-quote.net
Construction Material Calculators
www.constructionworkcenter.com/calculators.html
Building Cost Calculator
www.nt.receptive.com/rsmeans/calculator

Property Appraisal Information Online

Appraisal Foundation
www.appraisalfoundation.org
Appraisal Institute
www.appraisalinstitute.org
Appraisal Today
www.appraisaltoday.com
American Society Of Appraisers
www.appraisers.org
National Association Of Independent Fee Appraisers
www.naifa.com
Federal Appraisal Subcommittee
www.asc.gov
Real Estate Appraisal Books
www.rwm.net/books.htm
Appraisers Forum
www.appraisersforum.com

Property Valuation And Analysis Software Online

Z-Law Real Estate Software Catalog
www.z-law.com
Real Estate Valuation Software
www.atvalue.com
Real Data Real Estate Software
www.realdata.com

Tax Information Online

Internal Revenue Service
www.irs.gov

Internal Revenue Code And Tax Regulations Online
www.tax.cchgroup.com/freecoderegs
Revenue Ruling Bulletins
www.irs.gov/businfo/bullet.html
Technical Advice Memorandums
www.apps.irs.gov/news/efoia/determine.html

Lead-Based Paint Hazard Information Online

EPA National Lead Information Center
www.epa.gov/lead/nlic.htm
Lead-Based Paint Disclosure Fact Sheet
www.epa.gov/opptintr/lead/fs-discl.pdf
Lessor's Lead-Based Paint Disclosure Statement
www.epa.gov/opptintr/lead/lesr_eng.pdf
HUD Lead-Based Paint Abatement Guidelines
www.lead-info.com/abatementguidelinesexamp.html
EPA Lead information Pamphlet
www.hud.gov/lea/leapame.pdf

Building And Repair Cost Calculators Online

Construction Cost Calculator
www.get-a-quote.net
Construction Material Calculators
www.constructionworkcenter.com/calculators.html
Building Cost Calculator
www.nt.receptive.com/rsmeans/calculator

Reader Review Form

I want to hear what you have to say about ***How To Make Money Buying Pre-Foreclosure Properties Before They Hit The County Courthouse Steps***. I would greatly appreciate you taking a few minutes of your valuable time to complete this reader review form and write down your comments and suggestions about this book. Thanks for your help!

	Excellent	OK	Lousy
Organization of content:	( )	( )	( )
Clarity of content:	( )	( )	( )
Attention to specific detail:	( )	( )	( )

Did it meet your expectations?   ( ) Yes   ( ) No

What did you like best about it?_____
_____
_____
_____

How can I make the fifth edition better?_____
_____
_____
_____

Name:_____
Address:_____
City:_____State:_____Zip Code:_____

Please photocopy and return this page to:

        Special Report Publications, LLC
        322 Rio Vista Court
        Tampa, FL 33604-6941
        E-Mail: tomlucier@specialreportpubs.com

Special Announcement!

Now you can buy all of Thomas J. Lucier's books and special reports directly from the publisher online at Tom's new Web site, **Realestatepubs.com**!

Special Money-Saving Offers!

Buy Both Of Tom Lucier's Special Reports For Only $49.95 And You Save $10!

Buy All Three Of Thomas J. Lucier's Books For Only $69.95 And You Save $15!

Buy All Five Of Tom's Publications For Only $119.95 And You Save $25!

FREE Shipping On All Orders!

All books and special reports are always in stock, and all orders are always shipped for **FREE** within 24 hours!

Realestatepubs.com

Thomas J. Lucier's new Web site, **Realestatepubs.com**, is for serious, reasonable, rational, intelligent, goal-driven, action-oriented, reality-based adults who are willing to take calculated risks in order to make money investing in real estate.

The **How-To Articles** page has detailed how-to articles that provide real step-by-step instructions, and ready-to-use-information on a myriad of important real estate investment topics ranging from performing due diligence to estimating a property's current market value.

The **Real Estate Resources** page has one of the largest collections of real estate related links on the entire Internet! This is where you'll find reliable information on property records, comparable sales, foreclosure reporting services, property and casualty insurance, federal taxes, environmental hazards, lead-based paint, property appraisal, fair housing and other important stuff that real estate investors need to know about.

Aspiring real estate investors can take the **Real Estate Investor's Aptitude Test**, to "see if they have what it takes" to be a profitable do-it-yourself real estate investor.

The **Real Estate News** page has links to all of the major real estate news sources and real estate related trade publications.

Order Form

How To Use Real Estate Options To Control Undervalued Property: Everything You Need To Know About Real Estate Options: What They Are, How They Work And When To Use Them To Control Undervalued Properties With Immediate Resale Profit Potential! **$29.95** _____ copies.

How To Buy Used And Bruised Houses For Fast Profits: Step-By-Step Instructions On How To Find, Inspect, Negotiate, Buy, Fix And Resell Single-Family Houses For Maximum Profit. You Get The Lowdown On How To Profit From Dirty, Neglected, Run-Down Used And Bruised Houses That You Can Find Right In Your Own Backyard! **$24.95** _____ copies.

How To Find, Buy And Turnaround Small, Mismanaged Rental Properties For Maximum Profit: All Of The Nitty-Gritty Details, Step-By-Step Checklists, Sample Agreements And Realistic Advice That You Need To Know About In Order To Profit From Small, Mismanaged Residential Rental Properties! **$29.95** _____ copies.

How To Make Money Buying Pre-Foreclosure Properties Before They Hit The County Courthouse Steps: Complete Step-By-Step Instructions, Ready-To-Use Worksheets, Sample Agreements And No-Nonsense Advice On How To Buy Properties Directly From Owners Whose Loans Are In Default And Facing Foreclosure! **$29.95** _____ copies.

The Florida Landlord's Manual: Detailed Step-By-Step Instructions Along With Ready-To-Use Notices, Sample Agreements And Practical, No-Nonsense Advice For Florida's Do-It-Yourself Residential Landlords! **$29.95** _____ copies.

How To Quickly Evict A Residential Tenant In Florida: Step-By-Step Instructions, Ready-To-Use Notices, County Court Eviction Forms And No-Nonsense Advice On How To Quickly Evict A Residential Tenant In Florida! **$29.95** _____ copies. (Available November 2003)

Please note that all of Thomas J. Lucier's books are in stock and available for purchase online directly from the publisher at www.Realestatepubs.com.

Please use this order form to order books directly from Special Report Publications, LLC.

Method Of Payment: ( ) Check   ( ) Money Order

Please make checks and money orders payable to Special Report Publications, LLC and return this order form to Special Report Publications, LLC, Post Office Box 21283, Tampa, FL 33622-1283, (813) 237-6267.

Name:_____

Shipping Address:_____

City:_____State:_____Zip Code:_____